Literature, Cultural Politics and Counter-Readings: Hamlet as the Prince of Deconstruction

Literature, Cultural Politics and Counter-Readings
Hamlet as the Prince of Deconstruction

Anindya Sekhar Purakayastha

AAKAR

Literature, Cultural Politics and Counter-Readings: Hamlet as the Prince of Deconstruction

Anindya Sekhar Purakayastha

First Published 2020

ISBN 978-93-5002-640-3

Published by
AAKAR BOOKS
28 E Pocket IV, Mayur Vihar Phase I
Delhi 110 091 India
aakarbooks@gmail.com

Laser Typeset at
Arpit Printographers, Delhi

Printed at
Sapra Bothers, Noida. U.P.

To
Ashutosh Banerjee
who taught me *Hamlet*

Contents

Acknowledgements

This book is the outcome of my readings and research on issues related to literature, cultural studies and French post-structuralist thinking. Initial drafts of these essays were discussed with colleagues and friends and were presented at various academic forums within and outside India over the last one decade. I owe special thanks to Dr. Abbie Garrington who was my course tutor in the Scottish Universities` international program on modernism and postmodernism held in the University of Edinburgh in 2005. Her comprehensive discussion of Western critical theory sculpted my desire to explore further in this domain. I also thank all the library staff at the University of Edinburgh library, and central libraries of IIT Kharagpur, Central University of Odisha and University of Bonn, etc. for material support. Special mention is due to Ashutosh Banerjee who taught me *Hamlet* in the University of North Bengal and I dedicate this book to him and his class lectures which shaped my initial interest in the critical tools of reading.

Introduction: Texts, Counter-Texts and Subversive Reading Strategies

This book, as its title suggests, is an attempt at deconstructive counter-reading or at what Jonathan Dollimore called "creative vandalism" (2018) of existing cultural or literary texts. Deconstruction is a much maligned or should I say a much misunderstood word and in the Third World academia it usually bears a pejorative ring. While most of us would flaunt our familiarity with some of its philosophic jargons, for the majority, it is an area to be dismissed as intellectual obscurity or abstruse 'high theory' which is alien to postcolonial realities and hence to be abjured in academic practices of interpretation. My personal experience convinces me that there is an acute deficiency of serious engagement with deconstructive reading strategies and it has largely to do with our usual collective aversion to Derrida that emanates I believe from our lack of familiarity or engagement with deconstruction theory or with the philosophy of deconstruction. Simply put, there is a major dearth of Derrida scholarship and academics would grudgingly accept that, on the contrary they would weaponize them with ill-informed abuses for Deconstruction which as a philosophy has a deep political and ethical root. (Guerlac & Chea, 2009; Macquillan, 2007; Weber, 2012; Critchley, 2014; Phillips, 2016; Rabate, 2018). When Derrida is accused of abstract philosophical complexities, scholars generally miss out his central argument and his later and posthumously published works such as *Rogues* (2005), *The Beast and the Sovereign* (2009), *The Death Penalty Seminars* (2016 and 2017), etc. Like Giles Deleuze, Derrida goes against all forms of statist (authoritarian/sovereign) axiomatics and therefore any cultural materialist enterprise of re-reading literature and culture to understand the hegemonic structures of power in literary and cultural representations must adopt deconstructive counter-readings that subvert the hidden contours of power within traditional interpretive horizons. Such rebellious readings yield what Dollimore called 'dangerous knowledge' among readers that enables them to speak truth to power. Derridean reading tools de/re-historicizes a text to offer greater contemporary relevance of a literary and cultural text. Deconstruction acts as the saboteur, it perceives literature as an unique institution empowered with the Potenza for change.

Author as Saboteur: *Re-mattering* Literature at the Dusk of Writing

The singular signature of literature, says Derrida, lies in the noematic act of *evenement* or the iterability of the text that disembeds it from the given noetic closure. The Derridean idea of the *poematic* sees the poem/literature as the signature that allows its own dispersion, each time to fraternize a polytropy of valences. This book examines the *ungrund* of literature and related strategies of readings in the light of contemporary critical theory. The agonism between matter and *mythos* continues to elude a synthesis and therefore the mattering of literature has to engage with the heart of the matter itself. In other words, if literature and culture is to matter it has to be re-worlded in the current regime of materiality. I offer here reading tools to envisage such a *materialist poetics* in the aftermath of new materialist thinkers such as Catherine Malabou and Jacques Ranciere. Malabou's concept of *plasticity* and Ranciere's notion of *literarity*, I argue can re-manifestoise literature at the 'dusk of writing'. I also adopt Blanchot's plea for a revolutionary role of literature not in a reductive or essentialist mode but conceptualizing the rewriting of 'writing degree zero', semanticizing the structures of hunger and sufferings in a new language of plasticity that empowers language and thought with a new constitutive force to subvert the detritus of materiality. Such a materialist manifesto would definitely involve cross-borderal nomadism, enfolding the *Other*, attaining the *shibboleth* of dispersal as Paul Celan would say. A new literary pragmatics or reading strategy premised on larger interdisciplinary axioms to unearth the polyphonic nuances or signifying horizons of literature would fashion a new ontology of literature that neither gets reduced to a closure of literary bolshevism nor arrives at the complacency of an autonomous zone of isolation.

The *Cognitariat* and the Clamor of Being: Plasticity at the Dusk of Theory

The present volume, therefore, seeks to reinvigorate *theory* and *critique* through the optics of radical immanence or what Catherine Malabou defined as *plasticity*. Colonization of the epistemic life-world under the hegemonic logic of global capital has devoured all critical rage potentials in the cognitive universe and only a new metaphysics of Being can undo such cognitive imprisonments. Borrowing Negri and Hardt, I would argue for a Spinozian metaphysics of *radical immanence* that endows the Humanities with the constituent power of *living labor*, something which is gifted with *Potenza* or counter-power of resistance. What do we want today in the domain of Humanities education?—production of intellectual conformism or *resisting congnitariats*? The choice is between, *transcendent power* versus *immanent power, constituent power* and *constituted power, transcendent academy* as opposed to *immanent academy*. This book rallies for an immanent evental academy that would coronate the new Humanities of transformation. There is a lack of *plasticity* at the frontiers of Humanities, said Catherine Malabou and to restore that *plassein* it has to constantly reinvent itself. We have to choose between *Economimesis* or a *kairos-mimesis/plasticity*. The Humanities is to be envisaged as a discipline that determines the conditions and possibilities for a non-metaphysical plastic self-invention (Malabou, 2010). In the desert of non-evental times, under the hegemonic condition of profit-economy, the *impossible possibility* of a transformative humanities education can materialize through a sudden irruption of otherness into the mundane hustle and bustle of our downtown academia. We need a 'kairos moment', a moment of quickening time of difference, a *heterochronos*. One may refer here to Zucccotti Park, the liberty square in the aftermath of the Occupy movement and we need such constituent spaces of *kairos* or eventality in academia to fashion a gestalt of liberation in this non-evental times. The present book argues for a university as the *liberty square*, a space for the constitutive force of the Humanities and it does that through the empowerment of the sovereignty of the social collective or what Negri and Hardt define as the *Multitude* or the *Common*. Humanities as a discipline assigns to humanity the role of the subject or living labour, where *Being* is viewed as *Grund* or presence or an ontology of self-liberation, the *vis-viva* or creative life force. Let us open up then to a Negrian *Dis-ustopic Humanities* or *constituent Humanities* that draws a materialist project of insurrection to materialize the *a venir, the moment of the kairos*. Derrrida referred to the right to deconstruction as an unconditional right to ask critical questions and this implies the right to do it performatively, that is, by producing events, for example by writing, and by giving rise to singular *oeuvres*. The *new Humanities* would be capable of taking on the tasks of deconstruction, beginning with the deconstruction of their own history and their own axioms. The new Humanities can be defined as the "disciplines that determine the conditions of possibility for a non-metaphysical and non-scientific plastic self-invention of the human."(Malabou, 2010, 12) Such inventive and materialist parallax views would rescue theory from academic 'fiefdom' or professional abstraction. In what follows I shall explicate the inventive and materialist agenda of this book.

Fore-script/Sickle-script and Dis-bordering All Genre Distinctions

I prefer not to explicate further the exact scope and horizon of this work as that would preempt the reader to actualize her/his own ways of reading the book itself. However since an introduction is mandatory as part of any modular academic form, the question that I confront myself is how does one script a foreword/introduction to a book on deconstruction and literary-cultural musings? This question borders onto the metaphysical as it engages with the philosophical issue of signification and interpretive hermeneutics. To forescript, in a way is to foreclose the poetic/hermeneutic plusiverse into a unitary transcendental signified of meanings or a closed semiology of the text. The creative sign-system of a given text envisages the autonomy of narrative or effusive *gestalt* that constitutes the texture of individual *labenswelt* enabling plurisignification or the *jouissance* of multivalence. Then how do we legitimize the foreword, or an introduction? As stated earlier it cuts into the reader's autonomy, acting as Derrida would say, 'sickle-script', trying to meddle with the unique signature of the author and disarticulating/robbing in the process the pure creative rendezvous of the reader and the writer. All these deliberations are just to drive home the fact that to narrativize the writer's *oeuvre* or to chronicle the poetic landscape before the texts themselves is both a difficult and impossible job and the foreworder/introducer runs the risk of failing to do justice both to the text as well as to the reader. But then "What are the Poets for?"—asked Heidegger and the answer he amassed was disconcealment/'aletheia'. Was the author of *Being and Time* a poet? It is difficult to offer a straightforward answer to this question as the genre distinction between literature, culture and philosophy gets blurred and the porous frontiers of ontology and *dichtung* allow each other to cross-fertilize or to supplement each other. Hence the *dasein* of poetry and the Being of man spring from the same fountainhead and this parallelism permits the foreworder (who is also a reader in advance) to enact the curtain-raiser, to map ahead the ontological cartography of the given text. This does not mean she usurps the reader of her sovereignty or dislodges the poet's dialogic dynamics. The foreword is then a humble and self-effacing tribute to the text at hand and a coming to terms with its semiotic and semantic splendor, only to initiate the process of disconcealment, allowing the words to speak for themselves. This however entails an enormous amount of responsibility, as the onus of foregrounding the author and his/her poetic life-world must begin with trepidation and total humility, admitting in the first place the near-impossibility of the whole job. The author cannot be disembedded from the thoroughfare of her/his textual articulation. Having said that let me help the prospective reader to decipher the outlines and objectives of this book. It is primarily a work intensely preoccupied with the avowed mission of obliterating the borderlines between literature, cultural texts and philosophy. The essays here are deeply informed by Derridean philosophy of Deconstruction that empowers us with the critical wherewithal of counter-readings or engaged reading that challenge sovereign injunctions of literary, cultural or philosophical canons governed by traditional interpretive norms—such subversions are strategic so that fresh insights can emerge and we rediscover familiar corridors of significations with newer nuances of connotations and perspectives—something that helps in teasing out the dormant sub-texts, the rebellious anti-texts within the archaeology of a pre-given interpretive prison-house. Within the span of ten varied chapters, this book deliberately subverts categorical stereotypes like thematic coherence, linear harmony, etc as it coheres the apparently incoherent, weaves together obvious discordant subjects, as varied and staggeringly different as a Shakespearean text like *Hamlet*, Holocaust poetry of Paul

Celan, folk and tribal art, popular culture like film and media, Anthropocene and Post-humanism, Subaltern theory, Death Penalty and cultures of hate manifest in racial, gender, religious and caste-related violence, etc. What prompts me to force this co-living of these vastly diverse thematic within the cover of a single book is deconstruction itself, that allows the dismantling of all logocentric expectations of a single, continuous thread that serves as the traditional conceptual bedrock. The deconstructer is a saboteur, and therefore there is a claim for willing suspension of harmony in favour of an intellectual investment towards disruptive readings, readings that pushes the boundaries of subjects and texts to coronate ideas of anti-texts or counter-texts. My deliberate purpose here is to generate shocks and subversive amplitudes that expand the horizon of reading. Principles of deconstructive counter-reading/anti-reading/resisting-reading impel us to overlook the apparent disjointedness of the essays in terms of their themes. In a way this book is a constellation of several essays but what glues them together is the courage and adventure of innovative reading, a courage that enables the reader to situate Hamlet as a hermeneut, Deconstruction as the Jew of philosophy, Art as dissensus, popular culture as the slum dog syndrome, poetry as zooesis, and Death Penalty as psychic reimbursement of cruelty, etc. Such daring rebel-reading can even find affinities between Derrida and Ambedkar, between Hamlet and Karma philosophy, etc. This book therefore is to discover hidden affinities where hostilities are the received norms, it is a process of democratization of texts, and building cognitive and conceptual bridges across genres and themes through the hermeneutic of interpretation.

While incubating this book, I had in mind how the Mexican poet Octavio Paz described literature or poetry to be precise, as the 'Other Voice', a voice not sullied and subsumed under the hegemonic order of the everyday and the age of the spectacle. Blanchot's concept of 'anti-literature', terror of literature, Derrida's theorization of the 'strange Institution called Literature', and Ranciere's idea of 'democratic literature', etc were also the guiding principles for me while collating these diverse themes under the over-arching reading optic of deconstruction. Currently there is a widespread impression that something is rotten or wrong in the state of the Humanities and post-liberalization, literature is fast losing its sheen. Academia across the world are debating on the future relevance of Humanities or liberal arts education as humanities research is fast losing its currency in a world where everything is being measured by market value. How does literature survive or impact the marketized world of over-consumption and post-truth? The very framing of the interrogative sentence about the mattering of literature itself presupposes that literature is perhaps not 'mattering' anymore or that there is a growing skepticism about its effects in today's society of the spectacle. So is the literary space really getting diminished? To borrow, Walter Benjamin, are we having, the work of *literature in the Age of Readymade-Click-the-Mouse-always-already-Narcissistic-N-production?* The aura around literary and artistic texts has been eroded, now comes even the 'question of mattering'. The silent zones of creation and the salubrious ambience of the academy may continue to clamor for literary mattering, churning out tomes of journal articles and symposia, but the fact remains, the hegemony of the simulacra or the narcissism of self-enclosed entertainment and 24x7 info-topia cannot be subverted just by reiterating that literature is the Other voice or that it matters for reconnecting to affect. In a way this battle is nothing new. After all, down the corridors of history we have seen writers defending literature and cultural voices, and the battle today has got sharper, perhaps generating in the process more crippling forms of cynicism. Given that, the task ahead is action, an 'evental' break, an insurgent literature that scripts the 'prose of counter insurgency' against the biggest matter of all, neo-capital and its subsequent colonization of all domains. Forming micro-communities of literature and culture aficionados may help but what matters now are

Events, plastic new formations of dissensus and here perhaps the academy has the biggest role to play by aligning itself with activism or *avant garde* bodies. Failing which, the whole exercise of literature and cultural practices would remain futile and ineffective. The need of the hour is an alternative manifesto, another version of plastic literature (by which I certainly do not mean ideological politics, but mean it in a metaphoric sense of a rupture with existing trends), in other words, we need a literary and cultural spring and that can come up through occupying the public/capital space. If the age of the spectacle commodifies everything to matter, then we need perhaps tarrying with the spectacle to forge a counter narrative of literariness. This is no cake walk or conference room proceeding, it requires performatives and blueprints for action. This book is a humble attempt to reenergize literary and cultural studies by instilling fresh critical optics in interpreting literature and cultural practices. It tries to deepen this consistent onslaught of critique on our collective jaded sensitivities and cliched reading habits. It makes an attempt to demonstrate how literature and critical cultural studies can break free of everything, can counter-write, has the power of displacement. Derrida too points to the juridical and political power of literature, conferring to it the task of facilitating democracy. Literature is also a sense of dissatisfaction or a lack, a revolt against family, or society.

REFERENCES

Derrida, Jacques, *Death Penalty,* Vol. II: 2 (The Seminars of Jacques Derrida), Columbia University Press, 2017.

Malabou, Catherine, *Plasticity at the Dusk of Writing: Dialectic, Destruction, Deconstruction,* Translated with an introduction by Carolyn Shread, Foreword by Clayton Crockett, Columbia University Press, 2010.

Phillips, John W.P., *Derrida Now: Current Perspectives in Derrida Studies,* Wiley, 2016.

Rabate, Jean-Michel, *After Derrida, Literature, Theory and Criticism in the 21st Century,* University of Pennsylvania, 2018.

Weber, Elisabeth, *Living Together: Jacques Derrida's Communities of Violence and Peace*, Fordham University Press, 2012.

1

Hamlet, the Prince of Deconstruction: Ghostwriting the Spectrality of Justice and *Karma*

The whole of philosophy is only a meditation of Shakespeare. (Levinas, 1987, 79)

Justice in itself, if such a thing exists, outside or beyond law, is not deconstructible. No more than deconstruction itself, if such a thing exists. Deconstruction is justice. (Derrida, 1992, 35)

Deconstruction has seemed like an apolitical aestheticism, an indecisive dallying with texts without concern for the demands and decisions of the real world, dedicated more to analyzing discourse than to power, preoccupied more with puns than with politics. (Caputo, 1996, 125)

The instant of decision is a madness, says Kierkegaard (Derrida, 1992, 58)

Was Shakespeare a philosopher or can philosophy find in him a radical soul mate? Was he a writer whom philosophers would have saluted or identified with or can continue to identify with? Did the Bard of Stratford have any philosophical agenda or was he just a crafty playwright cleverly manipulating different philosophical commonplaces to generate incredible metaphysical halo in his textual practice? Critics probing *Shakespeariana* and its philosophic credentials would like to make us believe that Shakespeare mastered and subsequently appropriated Machiavelli and Plato in his dramatic discourse of political philosophy (Stuart, 2010, 8-9) and therefore the thesis gains ground that Shakespeare was not just a playwright but an original thinker of singular political and ontological insights. Anthologies such as *Political Shakespeare, Alternative Shakespeare or Shakespeare and the Politics of a New Millennium*[7] do testify the rich density of Shakespeare's textuality that allows plurisignification through deconstructive re-reading. Recent works such as *Shakespeare and Philosophy* by Stanley Stuart (2010) and *Shakespeare the Thinker* by A D Nuttal (2007), *Shakespeare's Philosophy: Discovering the Meaning behind the Plays* by Colin McGinn (2006), engaging with the issue of Shakespeare and philosophy, have unearthed the philosophic ramifications of Shakespearean texts and therefore it comes as no surprise when Derrida reads Hamlet as spectrally connected to Karl Marx and his legacy in his *Specters of Marx* (Derrida, 1994).

But then what is Hamlet doing in a book on Marx and neo-capital? Why is Hamlet exemplary for Derrida? What drags Derrida to Hamlet are two elements in the play, namely the figure of the Ghost and the notion of disjointure, i.e. the image of a world out of joint: 'the time is out of joint, O cursed spite that ever I was set to put it right'. (Jenkins, 1982) Both these two motifs converge on the ontological and the ethico-political, the metaphysical realm of being and the historical realm of justice and one can argue that the text of *Hamlet* provides Derrida the opportunity to introduce his theory of justice *a venir, or justice to come*. Shakespeare's attempted transcendence of the traditional notion of revenge in *Hamlet* allows Derrida the scope to grope for new coordinates of meanings in the play by his deconstructive reading of spectrality in *Hamlet*. Until now critics have focused mainly on Hamlet as an individual who is either a noble misfit (Goethe) or a sterile intellectual (L.C. Knights, Wilson Knight) but Derrida by explicating his theory of justice-to-come and his inventive interpretation of spectrality in *Hamlet* has challenged the very notion of a grounded closure of justice, thereby problematising the very idea of revenge (the central issue of the play) as purely futile.

The Ghost in *Hamlet* according to conventional interpretation either symbolized Hamlet's traumatized conscience or the devil. For Derrida however, it can also be a mark of ontological indeterminacy. I would like to argue that in the light of the Derridean interpretation of spectrality and hauntology, the Ghost, traditionally standing as the provocateur of revenge in the play, in fact helps in questioning the very idea of vindictive justice and what Derrida through his spectral logic consolidates or justifies is the prolonged existential or ontological dilemmas of Hamlet nullifying/deconstructing the potential of revenge as a final solution. This deconstruction of violent retribution and logic of punishment may even provoke us in boldly dragging Gandhi into the hurly burly of Elsinore which was on the throes of a bloody *coup-d'état*. Gandhi's philosophy of *Satyagraha or non-violence as* a tool of justice and righteousness is a far cry from the killjoy ideology of revenge but the Derridean interpretation of spectrality of justice may allow the seemingly absurd proposition of a non-violently violent Hamlet, a Hamlet-to-come, a Hamlet that could be, a Hamlet that perhaps Hamlet wanted to be. So did Hamlet, an heir of the revenge tragedy tradition in his brooding philosophization and hesitant conviction foreshadow the Hamlet, the master hermeneut or Hamlet, the prince of Deconstruction? The Bard of Stratford may or may not turn in his grave on mere hearing of such preposterous propositions and die hard critics may scoff at such audacious stuff as *reductio as absurdum* but there is no denying the fact that the future of Hamlet scholarship in the aftermath of *Specters of Marx* is bound to engage with such disturbing/deconstructive questions. Derrida has opened up new dimensions of the play *Hamlet* as it no longer seems a play where the protagonist dithers or a play of artistic failure or a play where the hero is a Freudian psychoanalytical marvel. Rather it looks more like a radical theatrico-philosophic treatise on justice, action/revenge and ontology of the rogue state of the 21st century. It appears more like a problematization of ontology than a tragedy.

The Derridean Ghostwriting of Hamlet

The reading of *Hamlet*, the Shakespearean play occupies the first part of Derrida's *Specters of Marx* but why did Derrida take refuge in *Hamlet* while deliberating his strategy of appropriating the legacy of Marxism for the twenty first century? The answer to this question can be ascribed to deconstruction's recurring preoccupations with the nature of justice (the ethico-political) and ontology (the philosophy of being). Derrida in the *Specters of Marx* invented the notion of the spectrality of justice and Being or of any such essentialised entities which have pre-given fixed structures. In a world dominated by sheer calculations and material gains, Hamlet, Nietzsche believed sees into the nature of things (Pendergast, 2005, 45) beyond local manifestations of injustice, some particular crime (like Claudius's) or forms of corruption (some thing is rotten in the state of Denmark) to something askew in the world itself, something radically and incorrigibly out of joint (Pendergast, 46).

As noted earlier, *Hamlet* then is exemplary to Derrida in two respects, one, the figure of the ghost and second, the notion of the disjointure, i.e. the image of the world out of joint. Both these themes converge on the ontological and the ethico-political, the metaphysical realm of being and the historical realm of justice. The figure of the ghost is the principal focus of the first two of these categories. The Ghost in *Hamlet* is distinctly Shakespearean as there is no ghost in the *Ur-Hamlet*. What Derrida makes of Shakespeare's Ghost is strikingly distinctive. For Derrida the significance of the Ghost resides in its radical indeterminacy. This however is not to be understood in terms of the normal theological reading particular to the Catholic/Protestant disputes of the Reformation, where the ghost is indeterminate, in the sense of ambiguous as to its provenance (Purgatory or Hell, the Ghost of Hamlet's father or an emissary from the Devil). In *Specters of Marx* it is indeterminate in the more strictly ontological register of occupying a place/non-place between presence and absence, appearance and disappearance. The specter is a "Thing" (Shakespearean term) and yet not a thing, not a substance. It hovers uncertainly between material embodiment and disembodiment. It inhabits a space of pure virtuality and what in that space is swallowed up is the ontological ground of Being itself (Pendergast, 46). Spectral is the sign of the displacement of ontology by what Derrida calls hauntology. Harnessing Shakespeare's ghost to Derrida's hauntology might seem slightly odd but Derrida's clever use of *Hamlet* is nothing but the first step in his innovative argument to align *Hamlet* with the deconstructive notion of justice and ontology. While using the textual fabric of *Hamlet*, Derrida moves from the metaphysical to the historical and from there to the ethico-political—that is, the question of justice. Derrida's rereading of Marx rests, fundamentally on a critique of the entrenched version of Marxism that locates justice historically in some material embodiment or other (the party, the International, the Proletariat, etc.). The figure of the specter is designed in part to remove and dissolve those metaphysical groundings (Pendergast, 45). The legacy of Marxism or for that matter any essentialized legacy of any redemptive ideology may, Derrida apprehends, congeal into the dogmatism of the ontological. So does the procrastinating Hamlet make an attempt to save himself from congealing into the dogmatism of revenge and justice?

The figure of the Ghost is also joined to another figure in the text of *Hamlet*: Unhinged Time, the time is out of joint. It is this link between the spectral and the disjointed that furnishes the crux of Derrida's argument; it is this paradoxical hinge, introduced at the very moment of speaking of the unhinged, that explains why Hamlet is so special to Derrida. In this crux, time, history and the world come together, all drawing towards a fateful question—the relation of action and justice, not just in particular historical worlds, but in the world as such. Justice and time go together by virtue of the former's determination by reference to a past and a future: on the one hand, an original wrong, evoking a historical causal chain leading back to a primary transgression, and on the other hand, a final rectification of that wrong, a final solution in which the historical, the political and the ontological will come together in a final moment of pure presence, realized in some form of material embodiment (Pendergast, 47). This is the conception of justice that Derridean deconstruction tirelessly exposes to critique. One of the grand themes of *Specters of Marx* is that the effort to establish justice by reference to an originary fault or crime merely triggers and endlessly reproduces the cycle of retaliatory violence (history as an endless revenge tragedy). The hint of anti-retaliatory logic of justice which Derrida seems to find in *Hamlet* strongly aligns Hamlet to Gandhi and his concept of *Satyagraha* or non-retaliatory non-violent violence. An ideology to establish justice by final solution merely installs the reign of tyranny. At both ends of the temporal chain, the political intervenes to impose a form of self-legitimating closure, called the just. Derrida wants to break this chain in the name of time as permanently and incorrigibly out of joint, disjointed, dis-adjusted, off its hinges, or spectralized, offering no site for the embodied manifestation of the just.

Given that, Hamlet's tragedy is, he is arbitrarily chosen to remedy the irremediable. In the final murderous scene of the play, vengeance and justice are finally enacted, but where has the justification of the just gone? Whatever it is in Hamlet's mind as he attacks and kills Claudius, it does not seem to be his father, of whom he says nothing and whose ghost has long since disappeared from the frame of the action. In a world of counterfactuals we could well imagine what the dying Hamlet might have said in connection with this question. Hamlet indeed seems about to speak, perhaps to explain his action as legitimate retribution, but of course he does not. The rest is silence and out of that silence arises the exploration of philosophic assumptions and possibilities of a new definition of revenge or justice.

From Hamlet, the Tragic Hero to Hamlet *a venir*

Does Hamlet, therefore, suggest the ideal/futural, the Derridean *a venir*? Some critics would call him the malcontent, a brooding inscrutable potential avenger, a wily plotter waiting for the perfect moment to pounce on the object of target, etc. but being emboldened by the Derridean insight could we treat *Hamlet* as a study of nobility or Hegelian *bildung*? Does it offer a glimpse of the preservation of nobility through enforced isolation? In answering the question how tragic is *Hamlet* we must begin by looking into the origin. The *Hamlet* story in Saxo and Belleforest is not tragic; it is a triumph of cleverness, of wit masquerading as idiocy. But Shakespeare changes all these and we do not—as we might in case of King Lear question the play's catastrophic end. What Shakespeare retains while cleansing the *Ur-Hamlet* of all the dross is the hero's differentiating intelligence. The mark of Hamlet's singularity is retained but it is transformed into a completely new kind of self-consciousness or self-hood. Eventually this singular self-consciousness of Hamlet, sometimes even referred to as solipsism, cancels out the force of circumstantial tragedy in the play, renders him in a deep sense indifferent to circumstance and hence action, and thus saves him or his self-hood from the crippling consequence of action. Hamlet is perhaps the one great Shakespearean tragic hero who suffers no loss of the self. From the very beginning he is uniquely conscious of his own autonomy and self-truth. This is evident in the famous speech on being and seeming, feeling and avowal, in a mourner:

> *These indeed seem*
> *For they are actions that a man might play;*
> *But I have that within which passes show,*
> *These but the trappings and the suits of woe.*
>
> (I.ii, 83-6) (as mentioned by Supriya Chaudhuri in her essay on *Hamlet*)

Hamlet's melancholia or his prolonged brooding on his tragic debasement, according to one critical view, does not make him a malcontent, on the contrary he "throws up an image of a spirit in 'self-estrangement' (*Der sich entfremdete Geist : die Bildung*)" (Chaudhuri, 1986, 25). But Hamlet's alienation of self turns out to be the smithy of his self-preservation. The nobility that characterizes the most highly developed form of free self-consciousness is a nobility of "being–with-the self or *Beisichsein*" (Chaudhuri, 1986, 25). For Hegel the entire phase of culture is a period of unhappy consciousness in which alienation is both inevitable and necessary. Under the discipline of this alienation (*Entfremdung*), the subject undergoes a formation (*Bildung*) which will enable him to win a higher degree of freedom. According to Supriya Chaudhuri, we may recall Keats: "Do you not see how necessary a world of pain and troubles is to school an intelligence and make it a soul? A soul that is destined to possess the sense of identity." (Chaudhuri, 1986, 26) The Ghost's revelation reinforces Hamlet's instinctive alienation, but also strengthens his sense of self, making him conscious of his own singularity, or singleness, as of his isolation and difference. Hamlet curses his fate as he is chosen to set things right, Hamlet the alienated soul is angry at his fate-ordained *avatar* of the redeemer because he is more for self-preservation than for a decisive act of avenge. His is therefore a noble failure/deconstructer, a Coleridgean hero who vacillates from sensibility. Mallarme was right when he characterizes Hamlet as a "jewel intact in the midst of chaos" (Mallarme, 1945, 302) and he continues to believe that the play lies mid way between the old drama of multiple actions and the future drama of the self, the Monologue. The initial sense of nullity and defeat in the play is replaced by an extravagant sense of self-righteousness by Hamlet. His world–weariness in the aftermath of the shocking revelations of the Ghost is balanced by his versatility and capacity for self-extension in the face of a debased and apparently stultifying set of realities. Hamlet's self-consciousness is distinct from the stoic self-control of Horatio. Hamlet rejects this stoic *apatheia* of Horatio for his own attitudinal ideology. Like Horatio he too would protect his consciousness from impertinent intrusions but unlike Horatio in spite of retaining the stoic lesson of reserve, he will not reserve the soul but would spend it. Hamlet is conscious that it is not just on Claudius but on the whole world that he seeks revenge, and that action is meaningless unless it can validate a noble view of life. The idea of the noble can only be realized through ambiguity, indirection and criticism and in free self-consciousness. This existential or ontological problem creates in Hamlet a deep indifference to the central action of the play, or a distrust of it, or preference of alternatives to it. In terms of the play, Shakespeare sacrifices action to Hamlet; in terms of the character, Hamlet prefers himself to action. In the subsequent sections I will show how this problematization or deconstruction of action/revenge links *Hamlet* to the great Indian epical theory of righteous action of *Karma* of a *Sthitopragga or an ideal man.* In the *Gita* which is a part of the great Indian epic *Mahabharata,* similar issues of justice and action have been debated to arrive at an ideal form of action (*karma*) or spectrality of action. In the next section we will see how Derrida engages with Hamlet in his *Specters of Marx* to deliver his theory of spectrality.

Derrida's Concept of Spectrality and Hamlet

A recurrent topos in contemporary discourse is to locate a "turn" towards the ethical in Derrida's later texts. *Specters of Marx* is a good place to start, since it is often regarded as the book that initiates the "turn" in Derrida's thinking, where he explicitly begins to address questions of justice. It is true that *Specters of Marx* to a large extent is a book on justice but what Derrida calls justice is not an ethical ideal. On the contrary, Derrida questions the very idea of an ideal state of being, which entails a profound reconfiguration of our inherited assumptions about the goals of ethics and politics. An important clue in this context is the phrase that reverberates throughout the entire book: *The time is out of joint.* This line from Shakespeare's *Hamlet* is the leitmotif in *Specters of Marx.* In the *Specters* book, Derrida reconfigures the understanding of the utterance, "the time is out of joint." Apparently, Derrida maintains that our time is "out of joint" and that we have to combat the disjointure in the name of a better, a more just society. The pivotal difference, however, is that the classical concept of emancipation—like the Marxist form of political critique—is tied to the notion that the ideal condition would be of absolute peace. While the world de facto is marked by violence, exclusion, and discrimination, one thus postulates that justice in principle (de jure) should put an end to violence. In *Specters of Marx,* Derrida pursues this argument in terms of an originary spectrality. A salient connotation concerns phantoms and specters as haunting, reminders of the victims of historical violence, of those who have been excluded or extinguished from the formation of a society. The notion of spectrality is not, however, exhausted by these ghosts that question the good conscience of a state, a nation, or an ideology. Rather, Derrida's aim is to formulate a general hauntology (*hantologie*), in contrast to the traditional ontology that thinks being in terms of self-identical presence. What is important about the figure of the specter, then, is that it cannot be fully present: it has no being in itself but marks a relation to what is *no longer* or *not yet.* And since time—the disjointure between past and future—is a condition even for the slightest moment, Derrida argues that spectrality is at work in everything that happens. The logic of spectrality provokes Derrida to speak of the 'unpredictable singularity of the *arrivant* as justice' (Chambers, 1999) and such innovative conceptualization of justice or time or history have to negotiate with our pre-given/inherited forms of values. For example, one may ask how to conceptualize history/emancipation after Hegel and Marx without falling prey to Hegel's/Marx's very philosophy of history?

Derrida weaves an answer to these questions with the warp and woof of *Hamlet* and Marx. He starts his analysis with the third scene of the first Act of *Hamlet,* in which Hamlet waits for the return of the ghost, his father. In this scene, Hamlet will see the ghost, the ghost of his father, for the first time. Yet, the scene constitutes not the appearance of the ghost pure and simple--it will quickly become obvious that there can be no brute sense-data of the ghost--for the ghost has already appeared the night before. He appears this time only by returning, by coming again. Derrida insists that the specter always *returns,* the specter is a *revenant*: "one can never distinguish between *a-venir* (the future-to-come) and *revenant* (the coming back) of a specter." (Derrida, 1994, 38) This scene then marks the appearance of the ghost, the return of the ghost, *and* the return of Hamlet's father in/as the ghost. As Hamlet will say (and Derrida will repeat often) the time is already "out of joint," for his father, the ghost, appears for the first time only by appearing again. The specter can only be considered *un*timely, and this untimeliness broaches the possibility of history, historicity. "Repetition *and* first time: this is perhaps the question of the event as question of the ghost." (Derrida, 1994, 10) But what Derrida refers to here as the "logic of the ghost," and what we can call a spectral notion of history, interrupts this timely movement of history because the ghost can never be located, placed, or fixed in time. Since the specter's appearance always turns out to be a *re*appearance, that very appearance can never be found within a timely conception of history. The untimeliness of the specter calls for an untimely thinking of history.

Derrida gives a name to the thinking that would work through this logic of the ghost. He calls it historicity or hauntology. To take seriously the notion that historical events might retain a certain ghostly or spectral quality requires one to reconsider the role of theory beyond merely its relation to past problems that history has given us to solve. Spectral history demands a theory that considers the ghosts of the past and the specters (and events) to come. In his other writings (Chambers, 1999) Derrida has made a subtle but crucially important distinction between the future as simply future present and the future as the yet-to-come, *a venir*. The future as future present is nothing more than a point upstream in the river of time, a point that will soon arrive and become present; it is the future as thought through a linear or dialectical conception of time. Of course, almost all conceptions of time and of history must contain some notion of the future, but a spectral history eschews the future present for an *a venir*, a yet-to-come, since ghosts might always return or disappear. One could say that specters are always yet-to-come, but the present tense 'are always' would rob the sentence of its sense of *a venir*. Thus, one might do better to write, *specters are always already yet-to-come*. Conjoining always and already serves to highlight the untimeliness of specters. (Chambers, 1999) In his discussion of *Hamlet,* Derrida argues this notion by writing *a-venir,* which the translators choose to render in English as the future-to-come. That is, *the* future to come, the future not in the sense of a future present but in the sense of a yet-to-come. L'a-venir, an untimely future.

Hamlet and the Spectrality of Justice

Moving on with Derrida's motif of the *l'a venir* I would now focus mainly on the futural and poetic performative dimension of justice, a form of justice that both Shakespeare and Derrida had in mind. Derrida has distinguished between law and justice. Derrida says,

> But justice is not the law. Justice is what gives us impulse, the drive, or the movement to improve the law that is to deconstruct the law. That is why I said that the condition of possibility of deconstruction is a call for justice. Justice is not reducible to the law, to a given system of legal structures... in *Specters of Marx,* I went back again to the Greeks, to the word dike, to the interpretation of the Greek word translated by "justice". I contested the interpretation by Heidegger of *dike* and *adikia,* justice and injustice. I tried to show that justice again implied non-gathering, dissociation, heterogeneity, non-identity with itself, endless inadequation and infinite transcendence. That is why the call for justice is never fully answered. (Caputo, 1996, 16-17)

Derrida seems to suggest that a judge, if he wants to be just, cannot content himself with applying the law. He has to reinvent the law each time and if he wants to be responsible, to make a decision, he has not simply to apply the law, as a coded programme, to a given case, but to reinvent in a singular situation a new just relationship, that means that justice can not be reduced to a calculation of sanctions, punishments or rewards. As Levinas said somewhere while deliberating on the definition of justice,

> ... justice is the relation to the other. (Caputo, 1996, 18)

Connected to such notions of justice is the definition of Deconstruction as "the relentless pursuit of the impossible". (Caputo, 1996, 19) Everything in Deconstruction is organized around what Derrida calls *l'invention de l'autre*, the incoming of the other, the promise of an event to come. Derrida is a renegade philosopher but he is also a responsible one. By the same logic is Hamlet a responsibly renegade hero, responsible to the futural notion of justice? Deconstruction pledges unlimited responsibility and Derrida does not want philosophy to be a sitting judge but rather a wanderer and a nomad, on the move, on the call, without the wherewithal to lay down its head, hastening hither and yon whenever the call of the other summons it into action. So the philosopher on Derrida's telling is not an *Aufklarer* who sits in judgement over all our judgments, a meta-judge presiding over our judgments. That is the seat the old Enlightenment seeks to fill. But in the new Enlightenment (Deconstruction), quite opposite is the case. For Derrida the philosopher is a bit of a "rag-picker" himself, looking for the bits and pieces of the Levinasian other (Caputo, 1996, 27). This deconstructive new Enlightenment puts responsibility (to the other) before rights (of the self), it puts heteronomy before autonomy. Deconstruction therefore is the affirmation of the coming of the other. Now the question is, is Hamlet procrastinating / deconstructing to allow the space for the other view, calling into question the *a priori* notion of justice and revenge? For Derrida, "Justice in itself, if such a thing exists, outside or beyond law, is not deconstructable. No more than deconstruction itself, if such a thing exists. Deconstruction is justice." (Derrida, 1992, 35)

Deconstruction then does not set its sights on justice as the goal or telos within a positive horizon of foreseeability—like a Platonic *eidos* or a Kantian regulative idea—which for Derrida is what constitutes the horizon of the possible. Justice does not exist, is nothing present, is no thing, is not found somewhere either here, in present actuality, nor up ahead as a foreseeable ideal, a future present. Rather "there is (il y a) justice, which means: justice solicits us from afar, from the future, from and as a future always structurally to come. (Caputo, 1996, 135) What Derrida means by justice in the typical unorthodox, exorbitant style of deconstruction, is the singular, the Abrahamic exception to the law, the remnant and the fragment that drops through the cracks of law (Caputo, 1996, 138). The singular is not a case that can be subsumed under the universal, not a specimen of a species, but the unrepeatable, unproducible, idiosyncratic. The notion of justice and singularity is articulated by Derrida in what he calls the aporias of justice. There is justice only if there is aporia, only if the way is blocked, only if we have run up against a stone wall. When the way is not blocked, then we are just sailing along, but Deconstruction and justice everywhere encounter a single over-arching aporia- that is created by the chiasmic interweavings of justice as infinite, incalculable, rebellious to rule and foreign to symmetry, heterogeneous and heterotropic. The infinity, incalculability and heteronomy of justice which goes to the heart of deconstruction may inspire a rereading of *Hamlet* on these lines of non-dogmatic, non-calculable (undecidable) forms of futural justice which Hamlet is perhaps half-consciously aspiring for.

Revenge and the Ghost of Undecidability

Undecidability then is not a vice and Hamlet elevates himself as a deconstructionist visionary through his undecidability and his inaction should not be taken to mean his pathetic state of apathy, his inability to act, or an utter paralysis. Instead of being a hurdle to act, undecidability is the condition of the possibility of acting and deciding. For a decision is really a decision when it is more than a programmable, deducible, calculable, computable result of a logarithm, that is because it has passed through the ordeal of undecidability. One way to keep this straight is to see that the opposite of undecidability is not decisiveness but programmability, calculability, formalizability. Decision-making, judgment on the other hand positively depends on undecidability, which gives us something to decide. Like everything else in Deconstruction, deciding is a possibility sustained by its impossibility. So a just decision, a judgment that is worthy of the name, one that responds to the demands of justice, one that is more than merely legal, goes eye-ball to eye-ball with undecidability, stares it in the face, looks into that abyss, and then makes the leap or gives itself up to the impossible decision. That does not mean it is decisionistic, for that would break the tension in the opposite direction, by dropping or ignoring the law altogether and substituting subjectivistic autonomy for responsibility to the other. One revealing result of Derrida's line of thinking is that "only a decision is just." (Chambers, 1999) The only thing that can be called "just" is a singular action in a singular situation, the warm glow of justice never settles over the law, the rule, the universal. But the definition of the Just must be continually invented, or reinvented, from decision to decision, in the occassionalistic and inventionalistic time of the moment. That is why Derrida speaks of the ghost of undecidability: for the undecidability is never set aside, never over and done with. It hovers over a situation before, during and after the decision, like a specter of justice, distributing it from within, divesting it of absolute self-assurance. (Derrida, 1992, 35)

Justice therefore is the welcome given to the other in which we do not so far as we know, have anything up our sleeves; it is the hospitality that we extend to the other or the other view, it is the expenditure without return, given without a desire for reappropriation, dispensed in a moment of madness, in which we tear up the circle of the law, in a time without time, in a desire beyond desire. Justice therefore is akin to the Derridean concept of the gift. Conventional law or justice is a calculated balance of payments, of crime and punishment, of offence and retribution, a closed circle of paying off and paying back. But real justice or justice to come and gift are impossible, the impossible which is our passion, our dream, the passion by which we begin and are impassioned. The passion for justice and the passion for the gift come together in and as the passion for the impossible. In *Specters of Marx*, Derrida pursues the impish paradox that justice happens precisely when the "time is out of joint," that the possibility of justice lies in dis-joining, dis-adjustment, a point he pursues by way of cross-reading of Shakespeare's *Hamlet* with Karl Marx which is itself a peculiar conjoining of the disjoint. Justice is dis-ad-justment and dis-junctrure. For only thus is there an opening up to the future, to what is to come, to the coming of the other and the justice to come. That opening breaks the spell of the present closure, allowing the present to be haunted by ghosts. Not only ought the living present to be disturbed by the spirits(revenants) of the dead, whose suffering justly claims our memory and mourning, but it also to be pried open by the ones still to come (arrivants), who also lay claim to justice.

Justice then according to Derrida is never found in the present order, is never present to itself, is never gathered unto itself. The essence of justice therefore is to have no essence, to be in disequilibrium, never to be adequate to itself, never identical with itself. Justice calls, justice is to come, but justice does not exist. The specters of justice disturbed the assured distinction between what is and what is not, between to be and not to be, issues related to Being about which we can be instructed better by Hamlet than by Heidegger. These futural and non-essentialist concepts of Derrida remind us of his notion of the messianic without messianism or groundless groundedness and these "prayers and tears of Derrida" (or Hamlet) (Caputo, 1997) vis-a vis the spectral visitations of existentialist questions border on the quasi-spiritual or poetic performatives and such traces of non-religious futural spirituality/ethico-politicality definitely provoke an alignment of Hamlet's spectrality with some Indian spiritual-philosophic coordinates. Hamlet's existential unrest assumes greater philosophic proportion through such deconstructive/ spectral reading.

Hamlet and the *Karma* Philosophy of the *Gita*

Hamlet resembles Arjuna in many ways in their identical melancholia and existential dejection over the task to set right the disjuncture of time. Arjuna is one of the central characters in the seminal Indian epic *Mahabharata* where *Kurukhetra* the battle of all battles took place for a decisive settlement of issues like justice and altruism. Arjuna the Hamletesque protagonist of righteousness abjures his bows and arrows just on the eve of the mega battle. Duryodhana, the arch enemy of the Arjuna camp vowed not to yield even an inch of land to his opponents without the battle of *Kurukhshetra*. Reacting to such antagonism, Arjuna who belongs to the *Pandava* clan is expected to gear up and brace himself to avenge all the injuries and insults unleashed by the *Kaurava* clan of *Duryodhana*. *Kurukhshetra* is the Elsinore of *Mahabharata* and Arjuna the valiant is expected to cleanse the land of *Bharata* (India) of the bloody misdemeanors of the *Kauravas* (Claudiuses). All the mythological Gods as depicted in the epic *Mahabharata* are favouring Arjuna and his side to vanquish the evil (*Kauravas*). But just when the battle is about to start, Arjuna drops his *Gandiva* (bow), he the valiant is suddenly engulfed in melancholy. He starts brooding on the efficacy or futility of war to settle scores. What justice, what righteousness is to be scripted on a bloody scaffolding? Just when the war fever reaches its culminating point, Arjuna deconstructs the very metaphysics of war as a means to establish justice and law. His dejection and scepticism is so overpowering that he vows not to fight again. Arjuna's drooping valor and hermeneutic dejection occasioned the injunctions of Krishna, the Lord who was officiating as the charioteer of Arjuna in the battle. Krishna intervenes and inspired Arjuna to stick to his commitment of righteous action (in this context war). The Krishna-Arjuna dialogue on the necessity of action or *dharma* constitutes the main part of the *Gita* (Edgerton, 1972), a text which was read and venerated by the likes of T. S. Eliot, Ezra Pound, Walt Whitman, Emerson and W. B. Yeats. The *Gita* is an intense ontological and ethico-political treatise on the right course of action in life. Krishna's excursus on the philosophy of confrontation/justice constitutes the central discursive praxis of the *Gita*.

The Gita and Gandhi's Interpretation of Revenge as *Ahimsa*

The idea of spectrality as suggested by *Hamlet* and as corroborated by Derrida was actually practised by Gandhi in his struggle against colonial injustice and brutalities. Gandhi reinterpreted/spectralized the exhortations of the *Gita* to fashion his unique vision of non-violent violence or *ahimsa* or true justice ungrounded in the philosophy of revenge. The *Mahabharata (of which* the *Gita is a crucial part),* a book full of battles and confrontations has not valorized the necessity of warfare; on the contrary, the book proved its futility. The epic has made the victors shed tears of sorrow and repentance, and has left them nothing but a legacy of miseries. For many interpreters the *Gita* is a solemn book to justify violence and warfare as a tool of justice but Gandhi, the apostle of peace reinterpreted the *Gita,* as an excursus on self-realisation through the practice of *dharma* (deconstruction). (Nadkarni, 2011, 61-76) The *Gita,* Gandhi feels, tells us how a perfect man is to be known. The perfected/noble man of the *Gita,* according to Gandhi does not substantiate the glory of physical warfare rather while dwelling on the ethos of revenge and action, the

Gita explains that Man is not at peace with himself till he has become like unto God/divine/ideal. The endeavour to reach this state is the supreme and the only ambition worth having. The object of the *Gita* therefore is to explore the most excellent way to attain self-realization through the renunciation of the fruits of action or *karma*. He who broods over results is like a man given to objects of senses; he is ever distracted, he says goodbye to all scruples, everything is right in his estimation and he therefore resorts to means fair and foul to attain his end. Gandhi says, "thinking along these lines, I have felt that in trying to enforce in one's life the central teaching of the *Gita,* (which is a treatise on war and revenge as righteous action or *karma*), one is bound to follow Truth and *ahimsa*. When there is no desire for fruit, there is no temptation for untruth or *himsa/ violence*. Take any instance of untruth or violence, and it will be found that at its back was the desire to attain the cherished end." (Nadkarni, 174) Gandhi therefore radically redefines the *Gita*'s philosophy of *karma* as the renunciation of fruit of action or shall we say of established definition of action or *karma*. The third and fourth chapters of the *Gita* read together interpret sacrifice, not as animal-sacrifice but as *sannyasa* or non-action (spectralized action). The *sannyasa* concept of the *Gita* will not tolerate complete cessation of all activity, rather the *sannyasa* of the *Gita* is all work and yet no work. Gandhi reminds us that "after forty years' unremitting endeavor fully to enforce the teaching of *the Gita* in my own life, I have in all humility felt that perfect renunciation is impossible without perfect observance of *ahimsa* in every shape and form" (Nadkarni, 177). The *Gita* is not an aphoristic work; it is a great religious poem and the deeper we delve into it (deconstruct), the richer the significations emerge. The *Gita* is not a collection of do's and don'ts. What is lawful for one may be unlawful for another. What is permissible at one time, or in one place, may not be so at another time, and in another place. Desire for fruit of action is the only universal prohibition. Desirelessness (deconstructiveness?) is obligatory. Would it be too much to relocate *Hamlet* in the Gandhian reading of the *Gita* which calls for abjuring the fruits of action or desireless deconstructed action and inspires us to aspire for futural forms of action or justice, attaining *justice-to-come* through a constant exploration/spiritualization/spectralization of the *action-to-come*? Derrida's specters of *Hamlet* pave the way for the *ahimsas* of Hamlet, paved the way for Hamlet waiting for the real "The courtier's, soldiers, scholars eye..." Hamlet-to-come.

REFERENCES

Caputo, John D., *Deconstruction in a Nutshell, A Conversation with Jacques Derrida* (New York, Fordham University Press), 125.

Chambers, Samuel A. Chambers, "Spectral History, Untimely Theory", *Theory and Event* online journal, Vol. 3, No. 4, (1999).

Caputo, John D, *Prayers and Tears of Jacques Derrida* (Bloomington, Indianapolis, Indiana University Press, 1997).

Chaudhuri, Supriya, "Hamlet and the Concept of Nobility" in *Jadavpur University Journal of English Literature*, Jadavpur, India, Vol. 5, (1986), 25.

Derrida, Jacques, "Force of Law: The 'Mystical Foundation of Authority,'" in *Deconstruction and the Possibility of Justice*, translated by Mary Quaintance, edited by D.G. Carlson *et al.*, (New York: Routledge, 1992), 35.

Derrida, Jacques, *Specters of Marx, The State of Debt, the Work of Mourning and the New International* (New York and London, Routledge, 1994).

Edgerton, Franklin, Translated and Interpreted, *The Bhagavad Gita* (Cambridge, Massachusetts, Harvard University Press, 1972)

Levinas, Emmanuel, *Time and the Other and Additional Essays*. Trans. Richard A. Cohen (Pittsburgh, Duquesne University Press, 1987), 79.

Lal, P. (Transcreated) *The Mahabharata of Vyasa*, (New Delhi, Vikas Publishing House, 1989).

Mallarme, S., *Hamlet, 1886 in Oeuvres Completes*, ed. H. Mondor and G. Jean Aubry (Paris, 1945), 302.

Nadkarni, M.V., *Ethics for Our Times, Essays in Gandhian Perspective* (New Delhi, Oxford University Press, 2011), 61-76.

Pendergast, Christopher, *"Derrida's Hamlet"*, *SubStance,* Vol. 34, No.1, (Issue 106, 2005), 45.

Stuart, Stanley, *Shakespeare and Philosophy* (New York, Routledge, 2010), 8-9.

Scott, Mallin Eric, "Review of Linda Charnes, Shakespeare and the Politics of a New Millennium", *Shakespeare Quarterly,* Vol 58, No. 4, Winter 2007, 558-560.

All citations of *Hamlet* are from the New Arden edition of Harold Jenkins (London, 1982).

2

Deconstruction, the Jew of Philosophy: Paul Celan's Poetology and the Dispersal of Logos

The effacement of the date or of the proper name inside the ring: here is the origin of philosophy, of hermeneutics, of poetics, their send off. (Jacques Derrida, 2005, 49)

In a language, in the poetic writing of a language, there is nothing but shibboleth. Like the date, like a name, it permits anniversaries, alliance, return, commemoration—even if there were no more trace- what one commonly calls a trace, the subsistent presence of a remainder, even if there were scarcely an ash of what one thus still dates, celebrates, commemorates or blesses. (Jacques Derrida, 2005, 33)

The poem wants to reach the Other, it needs this Other, it needs a vis a vis. It searches it out and addresses it.
(Paul Celan, as quoted by Derrida, 2005, 181)

For this reason, by way of its nature [von seinem Wesen... her] *and by way of its thematic, the poem is a school of real humanity: It teaches the understanding of the other as the other, in its being other. It demands reverence for this other, change of direction to this other.* (Eshel, 2004, 74)

Paul Celan would argue that poetry is a figure of the Other, and for him "the poem becomes the Jew of literature...One can Jewify [*verjuden*]...I consider Jewification [*Verjudung*] recommendable...Jewification that seems to me to be a way of understanding poetry" (Eshel, 68). Celan's observations intend to distinguish poetry as the linguistic realm that sets itself free from the restrictions of hegemonic discourse or semantic fixity. Just as the Jew was stigmatized / marked as the Other by his jabbering language, poetry is the radical *Other* to discursive language. By employing a mode of communication that remains 'the outcast' of language- the Other- the poem can confront the prevalent discourse that separates the self from the seemingly alien / Other. Celan's hermetic poetology advocates the doctrine of poetic *verjuden* or Jewishness of poetry which deconstructs the given *a priori* by opening up a space for the Other. As Celan says, "One can become a Jew, like one can become a human being; one can Jewify" (Eshel, 69). Celan therefore viewed poetry as a form of searching for one's self in the sphere of the Other:

> "*Verjuden*: It is becoming the other, becoming the other and his standing-secret [*Zum-anderen-und-dessen-Geheimnis-stehn*]..."
>
> "Turning back [Umkehr]- to do this, there certainly seems to be too many one-way streets. Moving against the traffic [*Gegenerkehr*]" (Eshel, 70)

Celan's *verjuden* codifies not only the experience of exclusion and persecution, but also the moment of becoming the desired Other. Celan significantly names this movement 'turning back' [*Umkehr*] (Eshel, 70). Unlike Heidegger's *Kehre*, Celan's *Umkehr* is a turning away from the centricity of the self, from care[*Sorge*], which is restricted to *Dasein's* well-being (Heidegger, 1947, 17). His turning back envisions a counter-traffic that opens multiple pathways and this concept of the 'turning back' is not a mere metaphorical rhetoric in his poetry, rather it looks at the poem as a linguistic field that turns towards time and the traces of history to invoke the Other and through this invocation of the Other something happens in the poem. In his 'Meridian Speech', Celan named this event of invocation of the Other, a turning of breath [*Atemwende*] (Eshel, 73). The poem is not for mere transcendent signification, the poem is capable of much more, not mere representation of fixities but the evocation of the Other qualifies as the *eidos* of poetry. Celan's poetology finds its philosophical counterpart in Emmanuel Levinas's philosophic preoccupation with the *other* and Derrida's theory of *dissemination, difference* or the philosophy of dispersal. In this chapter I attempt a discussion of Derrida's philosophic kinship with Celan's doctrine of poetic *verjuden* through an analysis of Derrida's study of Paul Celan's poetology in his book *Sovereignties in Question, The Poetics of Paul Celan* (2005). Deconstruction is not merely a radical method of reading and interpretation of a text but the deconstruction of texts is essentially and emphatically philosophical and political. I propose, first, to restate the rationale for deconstruction as a radical method of reading texts and, second, to indicate that this radicality leads Derrida to claim that deconstruction constitutes an entirely new way not merely of thinking but more fundamentally of constituting the world. As such, deconstruction necessarily has deeper philosophico-political consequences. Deconstructive readings and writings are not simply analyses of discourse, they are also effective or active interventions in particular political and institutional dogmas that transform contexts without limiting themselves to theoretical or constative utterances. Derrida's concern for the Other or the other/opposite view and his advocacy of *aporetic* dissemination and differential dispersion of the logos is also a kind of philosophic *Umkehr* or theoretic *verjuden* to Jewify philosophy by deconstructing the hegemony of presence. In the subsequent sections we would see that Derrida in his discussion of Celan's poetic hermeneutism in the essay 'Shibboleth for Paul Celan' has mentioned the opinion of someone that 'all poets are Jew' (Derrida, 2005, 50) as they open the singularity of words for the Other in their poetic discourse and by the extension of the same logic we may claim that the philosophical terrain of deconstruction also Jewify, opening the realm of signification to the Other.

Derrida's Suturation of the Poematic with the Philosophic

Derrida has sutured philosophy to poetry and his reading of Celan's poetology provides an alternative way of letting philosophy be guided by poetry. Derrida's approval of Celan's poetic hermeneutics clearly testifies the poetic orientation of Deconstruction as philosophy. His notion of the poematic is "the aleatory rambling of a trek, the strophe that turns but never leads back to discourse or to home. The poematic is neither a process nor a product, neither poesis nor work. It is an aleatory reworking, an assortment of paratactic phrases that manifests a desire *to be* rather than to represent" (Clark, 1997, 265). But in so being it makes no claim to the literary absolute. The poematic does not posit the work of a self but a dictation from the Other and as such it envisions a non-subjective work or an alterity-text where the irony of the signature signs the self to the other and the other to the self. Derrida's singular poematic "in the same stroke exposes itself to death and protects itself. The poematic never gathers itself together; rather it loses itself and gets off the track. The Derridian idea of the poematic sees the poem as the signature that allows its own dispersion, each time beyond the logos." (Clark, 235). In a similar vein, in his *Che Cose la poesia,* Derrida enacts his argument on the constitution of subjectivity through its deconstruction, its relation to alterity. Identity-to-self, as a structure of auto-affection, is necessarily constituted through otherness in a movement that prevents subjectivity being conceived except non-absolutely, as in impure difference, touched with a radical finititude. All such poetico-philosophic notions of non-absolutism and non-identity inform Derrida's theorization of a poetic-performative futural politics and philosophy. The present chapter intends to establish that the Derridian quest for the poetic-performative quasi-transcendental *a priori* that abandons all fixities and singularities have philosophic parallels in Celan's critico-theoretic preoccupation with the Other in his poetic philosophy. In the subsequent section I would discuss how a radical theoretic *verjuden* of the nonsingular emerges through Derrida's engagement with Celan's poetic domain in his *Sovereignties in Question, The Poetics of Paul Celan.*

Loss of Singularity, Inscription of the Invisible

Derrida's critical engagement with the issue of singularity/ logos in his essay, 'Shibboleth: for Paul Celan' consolidates his central philosophic concern for plurisignification and dispersed multivalence. A date in a poem may point to its poetic singularity and such a date presupposes the authentic witnessing of the poet's univalence embedded in the poetic fabric. Derrida shows how Celan has problematized the presence of the date in a poem when he spoke of the annulment of the singularity/logocentric presence of a date in a poem in his 'Meridian speech'. Derrida begins his essay on Celan with the remark that "circumcision takes place only once" (Derrida, 2005, 1) and then he continues to philosophise on the concept/interpretation of the term *one time* (*Uni Fois*). His contention throughout the essay happens to be how a philosopher of language or a hermeneut/poetician would conceptualize this notion of the 'one time' because the dating of a poem, the dating of an event in a poem gives the poem its sign of individuation or its singularity and this singularity may lead to an interpretive closure, barring the entry of the Other/plurisignification as the singularity of the date stands on exclusionary individual poetic authentication. Derrida clarifies that,

> My main concern will not be to speak about the date in general. Rather, I will listen to what Celan says about it; better, I will watch him give himself over to the inscription of invisible, perhaps unreadable, dates: anniversaries, rings, constellations and repetitions of singular, unique, *unrepeatable* events- *unwiederholbar* is his word. (Derrida, 2005, 2)

But the question is how can one date anything which does not repeat itself? How can one date anything other than that which never repeats itself? Talking about this question of unrepeatability, Derrida refers to Celan's poem, *A La pointe aceree* because this poem orients itself towards the *non-repeatable*. Derrida's theoretico-hermeneutic thematization of the date becomes more striking when he says that Celan's poetology has helped in the execution of a *mise-en-oeuvre* of the date. Celan in his 'Meridian speech' began by citing several dates but all these dates in Celan's 'Meridian speech' signify particular events experienced by particular people. Hence Derrida has raised the relevant question, who witnessed these dates? An individual who has signed the poem? The singularity and thematic veracity of the poem which is sustained by such singular dates that signifies the authenticity of the poetic event may also make the poem alone, singularity may lead to solitude as its singularity can only be corroborated and testified by the signatory alone. So, Derrida says, for the poem to stand and to absolve the solitude, it requires the secret of *encounter*. A date in a poem is its sign of individuation, its absolute property which poses itself as the sole preserver of the singular essence of the poem. Yet Derrida contends that this absolute property/essence/presence can be transcribed, exported, deported, expropriated, reappropriated, and repeated in its absolute singularity. This deportation or effacing of the singularity happens in its readability, otherwise closed by its singularity the poem may not speak. Yet Celan in his 'Meridian speech', Derrida reminds us, emphatically says that the poem speaks. For Derrida,

> ... despite the date, even if it also speaks thanks to it, as of it, of it, toward it and speaks always of itself on its own, very own behalf... in its own name, without ever compromising the absolute singularity, the inalienable property, of that which convokes it. And yet this inalienable must speak of the other, and to the other; it must speak. The date provokes the poem, but the poem speaks! And it speaks of what provokes it, to the date that provokes it, thus convoked from the to-come-of the same date, in other words, from its return at another date. (Derrida, 2005, 8)

So a poem speaks and it speaks to the date of which it speaks!

Instead of "walling up the poem and reducing it to the silence of singularity, a date gives it its chance, the chance to speak to the other."[18]

Dissemination of the Logos Through the Secret of Encounter

A poem has to absolve itself of the date so that its resonance may expand and move out beyond the singularity that may otherwise remain the sole property of the poet (signatory) and undecipherable, mute and 'immured in its date—in the unrepeatable' (Derrida, 2005, 9).To speak about the inscribed date in the poem the poem has to efface it, make it readable, audible, intelligible and disseminated beyond the pure singularity of which it speaks. Now this beyond of absolute singularity, the chance for the poem's exclamation or speaking, is not the simple effacement of the date in a generality, but its effacement in front of another date, the one to which it speaks, the date of an Other.

The singular and the unique or the absolutely personal in the poem must exceed it and such expansion alone can transport it and release it beyond its unreadable cipher. This expansion can happen through the secret of *encounter* or what Celan calls *Geheimnis der Begegnung* (Derrida, 2005, 9). Therefore through this process of expansion or *encounter* the singular date remains itself and also speaks of many other dates otherwise a specific singular date would remain closed and undecipherable to the other. Hence the encountering phenomena enables the coexistence of heterogeneous other dates under the single umbrella of the singular date. Celan calls this gathered multiplicity by a strong and charged name: *concentration* (Derrida, 2005, 10). Celan also speaks of the poem's Attention (*Aufmerksamkeit*) to all that it encounters. This attention would be the concentration that remains conscious of all the other dates, the multiplicity of dates around the same anamnestic centre, all the dates coming 'to conjoin or constellate at once in a single place: in truth in a single poem, in the only one, in the poem that is each time, we have seen, alone, the only one, solitary and singular' (Derrida, 2005, 10)

Polytropy of the Poetic Date/Signification

Celan's 'Meridian speech' is not only a treatise or a meta-discourse about the date/logos but it also philosophizes on the dispersion of the essence of the date through its, poetic *mise-en-oeuvre*, making a date,

> specific to the poet, a date for the other, a date of the other... a step by which the poet transcribes or promises himself in the date of the other. In the unique ring of its constellation, one and the same date commemorates heterogeneous events, suddenly neighbours to one another, even though they remain and must remain strangers, infinitely. It is ... the encounter, the encounter of the other, the secret of encounter (Derrida, 2005, 10)

The polytropy/multivalence of the poetic date absolves the claimed *a priori* provenance of the poem's singularity of the poetic signature or the poetic logos. Such a signification of the date may provoke the question, what is a date? Derrida here observes:

> the question " What is ...?" has a history, a provenance; it is signed, engaged, commanded by a place, a time, a language or a network of languages, in other words, by a date in relation to whose essence this question has only a limited power, a finite claim, its very pertinence contestable. This is not unrelated to the ... philosophical implications of Celan's work. Perhaps philosophy as such and insofar as it makes use of the question " What is... ?" has nothing essential to say about what dates from Celan or about what Celan says or makes of the date- which might in turn say something to us, perhaps, about philosophy (Derrida, 2005, 14)

Our conclusion therefore, on the inscription of a date in a poem, would be that what is dated must nonetheless not be dated. The date is there and yet not there. According to Celan:

> *Speak-*
> *But keep yes and no unsplit.*

> *And give your say this meaning:*
> *Give it the shade.*
> *Give it shade enough*
> *Give it as much* (Derrida, 2005, 14)

A date has to be marked off, in a singular fashion, detached from the very thing that it dates and in this demarcation, in this very deportation, the date/closed-signification becomes readable, readable as a date. Derrida contends that in the date the unrepeatable repeats itself, effacing in itself the irreducible singularity that it denotes. It is necessary that in a certain manner, the unrepeatable divide itself in repeating itself and in the same stroke encipher or encrypt itself. It must efface itself in order to become readable, to render itself readable in its unreadability. This is a clear parallel to Derrida's deconstructive philosophical rendering of differential signification where the fixed logo-centric presence of meaning is surrendered/ disseminated to allow plurisignification. The date functions like the proper name and acts like a password or shibboleth to decipher the poem. But,

> left to itself without witness, without a go between, without the altered complicity of a decipherer, without even the external knowledge of its date, a certain internal necessity of the poem would nonetheless speak to us, in the sense in which Celan says of the poem, "But it speaks!" beyond what appears to confine it within the dated singularity of an individual experience (Derrida, 2005, 17)

The date is compared by Derrida as the cut or incision that the poem bears in its body like a memory, sometimes a cluster of memories embedded in one, the mark of a provenance, of a place, of a time. To speak of an incision or cut is to say that the poem begins in the wounding of the date. But the date in the poem cannot come back in existence again, it remains as the spectral revenance, the date is the specter. The only way for the date to come back is to get carried away, transported; it takes off, takes itself off- and thus effaces itself in its very readability. Effacement happens through the merger with contrary events or dates. So readability effaces the date, the very thing that it gives to be read and this strange process is anticipated with the very inscription of the date. The date must conceal within itself the stigma of singularity if it is to last longer than that which it commemorates- and this lasting or this expansion or going beyond is the poem.

Derrida employs the term Shibboleth to give the full philosophic implication of the date in a poem. The date in the poem, according to Derrida, resembles a shibboleth giving ciphered access to a constellation of significations. Like a date, a shibboleth is marked several times, several times in at once. It is a marked but also a marking multiplicity as within the texture of the poem, it provides the password or the decoding mechanism, a sign of witness in all the situations along the significating borders configured by the poem. The shibboleth determines a theme, a meaning or a content but at the same time,

> as cryptic or numerical cipher, shibboleth also spells the anniversary date's singular power of gathering together. This anniversary date gives access to the memory of the date, to the to-come of the date, to its proper to come, but also to the poem –itself. Shibboleth is the *shibboleth* for ... that it commemorates others (Derrida, 2005, 25)

The analogy between Celan's poetology and Derrida's deconstructionist philosophy is evident when he says,

> Nor does it mean ... that to have the shibboleth at one's disposal effaces the cipher, gives the key to the crypt, and ensures the transparency of meaning .The crypt remains, the shibboleth remains, the passage uncertain, and the poem unveils a secret only to confirm that there is something secret there, withdrawn forever beyond the reach of hermeneutic exhaustion. A non-hermetic secret, it remains, and the date with it, heterogeneous to all interpretative totalisation. Eradication of the hermeneutic principle. There is no one meaning as soon as there is date and shibboleth, no longer a sole originary meaning (Derrida, 2005, 26)

Shibboleth and the Madness of the Date

The shibboleth therefore marks the principle of multiplicity/ *differance* within the very structure of language. Multiplicity within language or rather heterogeneity of signification leads to the *aporia* or linguistic impasse that distinguishes the poetic inscription which is marked by several significations within a single poetic act. The uniqueness of the poem, in other words its singularity of date and shibboleth, forges and seals in a single idiom, or in the single poetic event, a multiplicity of resonances.

Shibboleth, Derrida asserts, signifies that there is something of a crypt, one that remains incalculable; it does not conceal a single determinate secret, a semantic content waiting behind the door for the one who holds a key. The date (signature, moment etc gathering of singular marks) always operates as a shibboleth .It shows that there is something not shown, that there is ciphered singularity: irreducible to any concept, to any knowledge. A shibboleth then is the ciphered singularity that gathers a cluster of meanings and through whose grid a poem remains readable. The poem speaks even if none of its references are intelligible; none apart from the Other, the one to whom the poem addresses itself and to whom it speaks in saying that it speaks to it. Even if it does not reach the Other, at least it calls to it.

In a language, in the poetic writing of a language, there is nothing but shibboleth. The phenomena of *dissemination* are evident when Derrida says, 'We have spoken often of constellations: several heterogeneous singularities are consigned in the starry configuration of a single, dated mark' (Derrida, 2005, 35).

For Celan or for any poet, when they date, they name or cipher an event that they alone can testify or commemorate rendering the date encrypted. The date mentioned in Celan's words, "Nevermansday in September" (*unterm/Datum des Nimmermenschtags im September*") is quite significant. In this case a date becomes- from the moment it crosses the threshold of its surviving or revenance, from the moment, therefore that it crosses the threshold of the poem- no one else's date, *nevermansday*. If the name September surfaces in a poem, a poem that speaks, it lends itself to reading to the extent that it is caught up in a net of signifying conventions. Again therefore, the readability of the poem is possible through the loss of singularity/fixity/definiteness of signification. What is encrypted, dated in the date, is effaced, erased, the date is dated through its undatedness. That means nothing is encoded or encrypted in the date, it makes itself available to all. Derrida quotes Celan:

> *A date is mad, that is the truth.*
> *And we are mad for dates.* (Derrida, 2005, 37)

Circumcise/Deconstruct the Word

Effacement of the logos/date requires circumcision of the word. Celan has used the word circumcision not in the traditional ritualistic sense but to signify the cutting of the word, "*beschneide des Wort*", (circumcise the word) (Derrida, 2005, 39). Celan perhaps had in mind a different form of writing a kind of sickle-script (*Sichelschrift*) (Derrida, 2005, 38). This writing-sickle/deconstruction circumcises words in silence when speech is muted, so that songs may come. Dates/words have ashy existence, a date is mad, it never means what it says it is, and always more or less than what it is. It has no inherent essence/being of its own. Derrida refers to 'Singbarer Rest' which is the incipit or title of a poem by Celan that begins by saying the word 'remainder'. It begins with the remainder- which negates the idea of *being/logos/essence*.

A date is burned to become ash, but there is the glory of the ash, it consumes it from within only to preserve it and during the finite time of incineration, the password is transmitted to enable communication by circulating the shibboleth from hand to hand, from heart to heart. Interestingly enough, of a date itself, nothing remains, nothing of what it dates, nothing of what is dated by it. Nothing is possible to exist *a priori*. The annulment of the date, its becoming anonymous in the nothing, leaves its trace in the poem. The trace is the poem. Here we do not fail to notice Derrida's concept of the *trace* in relation to his philosophy of Deconstruction. What it comes down to is not simply the trace of something, rather it emerges or exists as a non-trace that happened, that took place once and asks to be commemorated. The trace in the poem is the trace of the date which erases itself to remain. It must expose its secret, risk losing it to eternalise it. It must, Derrida says, blur the border between readability and unreadability, crossing and recrossing it to extend the horizon of its signification,

If the date becomes readable, its shibboleth says to you: "I"(almost nothing, only one time, only once infinitely recommenced, but finite in precisely that, and de-fining repetition in advance), I am, I am only a cipher commemorating precisely what will have been doomed to oblivion, destined to become name, for a finite time, the time of a rose, name of nothing, voices of no one, name of no one: ash (Derrida, 2005, 41)

It is evident then that the date represents the poem's theme rather than its signature. For Derrida, the poem belongs to the date that it blesses; it gives and gives back again the date to which it at one and the same time belongs and is destined. The border between the poem's external circumstances, its empirical date and its internal genealogy is blurred. This genealogy is dated, that means that it is not an essential universal, atemporal movement. A shibboleth also crosses this border for a poetic date, for a blessed date, the difference between the empirical and the essential, between contingent exteriority and necessary intimacy no longer has any place. This non-place, this utopia is the taking place or the event of the poem.

The Poematic and the Philosophic

Derrida's supposed alignment between poetry and philosophy is built on this blurring of the external factuality and internal genealogy of the poem. With this distinction between the empirical and the essential, a limit is blurred, and Philosophy finds itself, finds itself again in the vicinity of the poetics, indeed of literature. It finds itself again there, for the indecision of this limit is perhaps what is most thought provoking. It finds itself again there; it does not necessarily lose itself there. It is the philosophical experience which is the questioning traversal of limits, uncertainty as to the border of the philosophical field- and above all the experience of language, always just as poetic, or literary as it is philosophical (Derrida, 2005, 44)

A poem is something that stands open and it makes its way through time, it is never timeless. Wherever a signature has cut into an idiom, leaving in language the trace of an incision, the memory of an incision at once unique and iterable, cryptic and readable, there is date. It is not the absolute date, there is no absolute date and absolute poem, but there is something of the date, the madness of the when, the *wann/Whahnsinn* (Derrida, 2005, 48), the terrifying ambiguity of the shibboleth. But the voice of the poem carries beyond the singular cut. The cut becomes readable for certain of those who have no part in the event or the constellations of event consigned to it, for those excluded from partaking, yet who may thus partake and impart.

Derrida believes that within the bounds of this generality or this universality, insofar as its meaning is repeatable in this way, a poem acquires the value of a philosopheme. It may offer itself to the work of a hermeneute that does not require for its internal reading, access to the singular secret known only to a certain number of witnesses or participants. The poem itself is already such a hermeneutic event, its writing is a matter of *hermeneuein*, and it proceeds from it. Looking at it from the side of the universal meaning that corresponds to the date, to that in it which might come again, in a publicly commemorated recurrence, one may always speak of philosophical implications. Philosophy, hermeneutics and poetics can only come about in idioms, in languages, in the body of events and dates of which one could not say that any meta-linguistic or meta-historical overview is possible—though such an overview is ensured from within by the structure of marking off that pertains to the iterability of a date, that is to say to its essential annulment. The effacement of a date or of the proper name marks the origin of philosophy, of hermeneutics and of poetics.

Opening of the Word for the Other

Deliberating on the thematic of the date, Derrida comes to the issue of Judaism, saying that Judaism 'has the same structure as that of the date' (Derrida, 2005, 49). That means when someone says 'we Jews', does it signify the reappropriation of an essence, or the sense of a partaking? The answer is yes and no at the same time. The Jew is also the other, the Jew is the other who has no essence, who has nothing of his own or whose own essence is to have none. 'All Poets are Jews', said someone, but that does not signify that the word Jew, shares one common covenant. Jew is the shibboleth. It is witness to the universal, but as absolute, dated, marked, incised, caesured singularity- as the other and in the name of the other. If we witness the universal as absolute singularity, as the other and in the name of the other, of the stranger, of you towards whom I must take a step that without bringing me nearer to you, without exchanging me for you, without being assured a passage, lets the word pass and assigns us, if not the one, at least to the same. We were already assigned to it, dwelling under the same trade-wind. Let the word pass through the barbed-wire order. The passage of the other, towards the other... respects the otherness of the other (Derrida, 2005, 51)

This philosophy of dispersal and non-essentialism of Derrida finds a poetic alliance in Celan's words:

> *Were I like you. Were you as I*
> *Did we not stand?*
> *Under one trade-wind?*
> *we are strangers* (Derrida, 2005, 51)

Respect for the Other is evident again in the following lines of Celan,

> *To a mouth*
> *For which it was one of a thousand*
> *I lost-*
> *I lost a word*
> *That had remained with me:*
> *Sister.*
> *To*
> *The worship of many gods*
> *I lost a word that was looking for*
> *Me:*
> *Kaddish* (Derrida, 2005, 52)

This loss of the word in the process of opening it to the other in fact suggests the loss of the origin and Derrida's own observation in this regard is worth mentioning, Spectral errancy of words. This revenance does not befall words by accident, following a death that would come to some or spare others. All words, from their first emergence partake of revenance. They will always have been phantoms, and this law governs the relationship in them between body and soul... what is called poetry or literature, art itself... is perhaps only an intense familiarity with the ineluctable originarity of the specter. One naturally translates it into the ineluctable loss of the origin (Derrida, 2005, 53)

In connection with this topic of the loss of the origin, Derrida mentions Celan's notion of *Beschneidung* or circumcision. As mentioned earlier, Celan however has used the word circumcision in a different sense, signifying the circumcision of the word. Derrida says that to claim that all the poets are Jews is to state something that marks and annuls the marks of a circumcision. It is tropic. All those who deal with or inhabit language as poets are Jews—but in a tropic sense. In fact Celan had a different idea when he said, "*beschneide das Wort*", i.e. it concerns the circumcision of the word. This word to be circumcised can be understood once it is circumcised as an open word and all those poets whom we consider as the Jew opens the word,

> *TO ONE, WHO STOOD BEFORE THE DOOR, one*
> *Evening*
> *To him*
> *I opened my word* (Derrida, 2005, 58)

This suggests the bearing of a word for the other. The word to be circumcised is above all, opened, like a door, offered, given, or at least promised to the other. The other remains indeterminate—unnamed in the poem. He has no identifiable face, he simply has a face since he must see the door and receive the word, even if this face remains invisible. Celan makes this theme of the opening of the word more clear,

> *To him*
> *I opened my word*
> ...
> *For this one-*
> *Circumcise the word,*
> *For this one-*
> *Circumcise the word*
> *For this one*
> *Write the living*
> *Nothing in the heart,*
> *For this one*
> *Spread the two*
> *Cripplefingers in the hal-*
> *lowing sentence*
> *for this one* (Derrida, 2005, 60)

This word of opening permits one to pass through the doorway. It is yet another shibboleth, the shibboleth at the origin of all the others, yet still one among others in a given language. The shibboleth is given or promised by 'me' to the singular other so that he may partake of it and enter through the doorway, across the line, the border, the threshold.

The poem becomes a poem by turning toward the Other. The hyper majesty of *Dichtung* and poetic *Atemwende* establish the philosophy of *Othering*, the philosophy of dissemination. Perhaps Derrida's notion of *democratie a venir* (i.e. democracy-to-come) (Chea, 2009, 81) refers to the realization of a*n* emancipatory futural quasi-transcendental telos by abandoning all forms of critical/philosophical dogmatics/singularities/logos. Derrida in his post-ethical *kehre* (Critchley, 2004, 99) phase envisaged a new form of critique which is hyper critical, a critique which is open to its own transformation/dispersal. Such a radical critique goes beyond the singular transcendental imperatives. The neo-Derridian approval of infinite responsibility for the *Other* (hospitality) or the quest for a non-deconstructionable yet non-absolutist idea of justice is without any fixed ground or *terra·*. Derrida's deconstructive manifesto is legislative without legislation. It is messianic without a messianic *a priori*. It recognizes the normative ground but redefines it and calls for a poetic- performative critique which is located in the poetic/futural *khora*. (Morris, 2004, 241)

REFERENCES AND NOTES

Celan, Paul, *The Meridian* (translated by Jerry Glenn, appeared in *Chicago Review*, ed. By Joel Golb,29,no.3, 1978:29-40).This essay appears as an appendix in Jacques Derrida's *Sovereignties in Question, The Poetics of Paul Celan*, Edited by Thomas Dutoit and Outi Pasanen (New York, Fordham University Press, 2005), 181.

Clark, Timothy, *The Theory of Inspiration: Composition as a Crisis of Subjectivity*, (Oxford, Manchester University Press, 1997), 265.

Chea, Pheng, *The Untimely Secret of Democracy in Derrida and the Time of the Political*, Pheng Chea and Suzanne Guerlac, ed. (Durham and London: Duke University Press, 2009), p. 81.

Critchley, Simon, 'Frankfurt Impromptu-Remarks on Derrida and Habermas' in Lasse Thomassen Ed. *The Derrida Habermas Reader*, (Chicago: University of Chicago Press, 2004), p. 99.

Derrida, Jacques, *Sovereignties in Question, The Poetics of Paul Celan*, Edited by Thomas Dutoit and Outi Pasanen (New York, Fordham University Press, 2005), 49. [All the references to Derrida's study of Celan are from this book. I have tried to locate the whole discussion mainly within the framework of Derrida's essay

'Shibboleth: For Paul Celan', which is the first essay of this book. However the central critical thrust of my essay has also been formulated on the basis of my reading of other essays such as 'Poetics and Politics of Witnessing', 'Majesties' and the two interviews of Derrida contained in the book.]

Eshel, Amir, 'Paul Celan's Other: History, Poetics and Ethics', *New German Critique*, No. 91, Special Issue on Paul Celan (Winter, 2004), 74.

[Heidegger rarely uses the term *Kehre*. He does so in his seminal essay *Uber den Humanismus* (Frankfurt/Main: Klostermann, 1947), 17.]

Morris, Martin, 'Between Deliberation and Deconstruction: The Condition of Post-national Democracy' in Lasse Thomassen ed. *The Derrida Habermas Reader* (Chicago: University of Chicago Press, 2004), p. 241.

3

Postcolonial Biopower: Politics of the *Nation-ed* and Dismemberment of the Other

> *The soul is to the body what the master is to the slave.*
> (Aristotle as quoted by Agamben, 2016, 4)

> *Ergon anthropou psyches energeia kata logon*
> *Ergon (doulou) he tou somatos chresis*
> [The work of the human being is the being-in-action of the soul
> According to the logos
> The work of the slave is the use of the body]
> (Aristotle as quoted by Agamben, 2016, 4)

> *Power in this instance was essentially a right of seizure: of things, time, bodies, and ultimately life itself; it culminated in the privilege to seize hold of life in order to suppress it ... one would have to speak of bio-power to designate what brought life and its mechanisms into the-realm of explicit calculations and made knowledge-power an agent of transformation of human life.* (Foucault, 1978, 136; 143)

This chapter engages with recent incidents of state control and state regimentation in India on the question of nation and nationalism. The pedagogies of nationalism within and outside India have a history of body control or what Giorgio Agamben calls the 'uses of bodies, (Agamben, 2016). Within the convoluted paradigm of nation and narration various templates of body use have been noticed that include extracting body labor or enslavement, body-precarities, tortures, etc. I decided to begin this deliberation on (corpo) reality with Aristotle's definition of the slave, as pointed out by Giorgio Agamben in his new book, *The Use of Bodies: Homo Sacer IV* (2016) as "the being whose work is the use of the body." (Agamben, 2016, 4) This inscription of the slave/subaltern within the coercive biopolitical network of bodily subjection is crucial for the line of argument that I am going to develop in the following segments and in my argumentative schema I decided to skip the all too familiar debate around the Cartesian mind-body dualism as, borrowing Foucault and subsequently Giorgio Agamben, I would argue, that the pervasive presence of the body as a site of sovereign execution of power makes the body an always already productive philosophical signifier and seen through that angle then, the body is central to my understanding of history, nation and the mechanisms of modern power. Tim Crane and Sarah Patterson in their *History of the Mind Body Problem* (2002) discussed in detail Aristotle's theorization of *De Anima* (On the Soul) which is classified generally as *hylomorphism* that views the soul as "the form of the body's matter" (Crane and Patterson, 2002, 3). The body in that view is perceived as "ensouled matter" as the soul according to Aristotle imposes a form on the matter of the body. Crane and Patterson inquired whether we should view such Aristotelian hypothesis as a materialist perspective or a dualist view or whether it can be classified as neither of the two and hence the debate continues even today and looking at the classical history of the mind body problem from a distance we can locate, according to Crane and Patterson, three very different paradigmatic strands—Aristotelian, Cartesian and Scientific Materialist (physicalist) paradigms. I would consciously shy away from these metaphysical debates and drawing on Aristotle's position on a completely different subject—slavery—I would focus on an alternative way of minding the body. I prefer to call it the biopolitical and deconstructive perception of the mind-body co-relation which is lacking in the classical mind-body problematic.

Body's intertwinement with the ideological state apparatus and the *nomos* of sovereign power also corroborates how it plays a central role in the constitution of dissidence too. Hence "constituted subjects" generate the "constituent subjects" or the agents of 'inoperativity' as well. Here I use the two terms "constituted subjects" and "constituent subjects" in the light of Agamben's use of the notion of "constituted power" (state or sovereign power) and "constituent power" (revolutionary or dissident potential). The *precariat* (Standing, 2014) or the old/new slave-subaltern is always denied every right so that s/he can be reduced to her/his "bare life" of the bodies and hence the uses of bodies have dual implications, one of subjection and the other of dissidence. The *homo sacer* (I take the liberty here to interpret Agamben's notion of the *homo sacer* and Guy Standing's idea of the *precariat* in simplistic and extended ways as the bare life of the slave-subaltern) has only got his bare body which is the locus of both constituted coercion and constituent outrage. I would love to build on this logic of the dichotomy between *constituted* and *constituent power* to organize my thoughts on the body. In the course of my argument I would discuss how the bodies of "gendered subalterns" of Mahasweta Devi's stories such as Draupadi and Jashoda play out this dual impact of bodily torture and bodily resistance. Any discussion on the subjection of the body however ultimately leads to the absolute form of body destruction, i.e. death penalty and in his last posthumously published work, *Death Penalty* (2014), Derrida exactly did that and went to the extent of saying that "deconstruction is nothing but the deconstruction of death penalty". My readers, I hope, would not mind this necessary detour to the realm of convicted dead bodies, which are mindfully ordained to be legally slaughtered to "satisfy public demand" or to justify "national interests" and in my work plan, body and penology or the juridical normative dismemberment of the body emerges as the conceptual pivot as I weave our contemporary reading of Foucault, Derrida and Agamben on the question of body/

bare life and biopolitical control. I bracket the convict and the subaltern or shall I say, the categorical triad of *convict-subaltern-precariat* (emphasis mine) as the locus of my analysis of the body and I would argue that the best way to do justice to the question of minding the body is to revisit the socio-political injunctions and subjections of the body that got philosophical endorsement since the classical age. In this case I would refer to the Aristotelian hypothesis of slavery (already referred to in the epigraph of this essay) and Derrida's exasperation at philosophy's continued silence (support) on death penalty to establish how since its inception philosophy has justified the exclusion and subjugation of the bodies of the deviants.

Coercing Dissident Bodies: Bare Life of the *Convict-Subaltern-Precariat*

In fact any genealogical attempt to study power yields a history of subjected bodies and when we look around today and see the dead body of a refugee child swept ashore in Turkey, bodies of beheaded terror captives, body of a lynched Muslim old man in India who was allegedly eating beef, bare bodied Dalits chained and being beaten, surreptitiously buried body of the hanged death penalty convict, the blood-stained bodies of Maoists or Terrorists killed in alleged fake encounters, etc, how do we demarcate the body from the mind in these mindless spree of human torture and killings? In this universally normativized festival of body tortures and the theatre of state brutalities, we can`t help minding the body. In other words, the sovereign urge for state/nation formation and territorial bordering can only be possible through a severe command over the docile or disciplined bodies of the subjected *other* and hence there is no escape from our minding the body as we meander through our civilisational history of national identity and rule formations. I plan to flesh out my reading of the bare life of the *convict-subaltern-precariat* through the Foucauldian idea of biopower, Agamben's notion of the *Homo Sacer*, Derrida's reading of Death Penalty and Mahasweta

Devi's writings on the "Gendered Subaltern" and I would draw my conclusion on how the body has become the primary signifier in our recent times in the debates centering around nation and nationalism. I intend to see how in the "imaginary maps" of nationalism we have fashioned a bloody body politic that coerces/biopowerizes the bodies of the dissident as anti-national. A whole body of thought emanates from here and in what follows I would first dwell on Agamben's genealogical study of the body in his theorization of the *Homo Sacer* and the use of bodies in Western political philosophy. Subsequently I would look into Foucault's analysis of body and punitive practices, Mahasweta Devi's discussion on the body of the gendered subaltern and Derrida's philosophisation on death penalty. In that way I argue we can at least address some important segments of the process of minding the body in today's context of ultra-nationalism when anyone can be ostracized as an anti-national if s/he does not toe the official line of nation and narration. Given the fact that in India or even in the Western world, pedagogies of xenophobia and hate speech have constituted in the last few years a politics of Nation which is sustained by Islamophobia, and hatred for the precariat/immigrant and the liberal-progressive, etc. Borrowing Partha Chatterjee one may even say that there appears to be a politics of the nation-ed surfacing in various parts of the world where majoritarianism and neo-fascist ideologies are being promoted in the name of nation and this politics of nation legitimizes coercive governmental technologies to control the nation-ed—lynch mobs and vigilante groups lynching minorities in India, the Myanmar state and military junta violating the bodies of the Rohingyas, Islamophobia leading to stabbing of a Muslim in a public train in broad day light, Body persecution of Dalits by upper castes in India, killing of rationalists and bloggers in Bangladesh and India, bodily humiliation of dissidents and deviants—all these are instances of dismemberment of the Other, an act of biopower evidently promoted by official politics of nation. This chapter narrates this national mode of coercive politics and at the same time hints at the constitutive power of possible counter-politics of the nation-ed. I will argue that the postcolonial state in its recourse to forms of biopower in which lynch mobs and vigilante groups are given virtually free hands to violate the bodies of the religious/caste/ethnic/epistemic/political Other generates a new form of national politics and postcolonial national biopower in which one section of the national population calibanized the other section in the name of nation. I would argue that this postcolonial biopower has actualized its bio-political jurisprudence on the triad of *convict-subaltern-precariat,* relegating every dissident or Otherized voices in the domain of precarity. A politics of the nation-ed is in the offing. In what follows I shall discuss theoretically such traditions of enslavement or precarity-making through a study of Agamben's book on *Homo Sacer IV*.

Agamben and the Use of Bodies

Giorgio Agamben in his recent work, *The Use of Bodies: Homo Sacer IV* (2016) notes how Aristotle mentioned the expression "the use of the body" in the beginning of his work *Politics*. In the same breath he recounts that while talking about 'families' Aristotle defined "three types of family relations",— the despotic relation (Master Slave), the matrimonial and the parental and while the last two relations are nameless, the first category is the one that prompts him to define the slave. For Aristotle, a slave is the one who "while being human is by its nature of another and not of itself."(Agamben, 2016) We shall see later how Mahasweta Devi's gendered subaltern in her stories exactly fit into this definition of slaves. Jashoda the hired milk-mother in the story "Breast Giver" milks her owner's grandchildren so that the wives of her owner's sons can remain beautiful and stress free. This breast labour on the part of Jashoda entraps her into a bodily form of slavery. Aristotle went to the extent of asking if "slavery is by nature contrary to nature." The answer to this question leads us to the category of "command" and the binaric relation of the "command and the commanded" which entails a lot of political economic configurations and here Agamben shows how Aristotle brings in the relation of the body and the soul to explicate his idea of the command

> The soul commands the body with a despotic command... the same must therefore also happen among human beings. (Agamben, 2016, 9)

Such despotic commands rely on a strategic economy of body coercion technologies and all that we do during such body tortures, is to witness these prolonged and legitimized forms of physical barbarity in a world structured through socio-juridical norms of body control. Borrowing Agamben can we call such acts of body coercion, the Auschwitz legacy? If we are to believe Agamben then Western politics since the Second World War (something postcolonial nations are perhaps replicating today) has been inscribed in the ideology of the concentration camps but the question is who were/are the victims and the witnesses of the camps? Agamben calls the witnesses of the camps, the "non-man" and this prompts us to inquire if they are the beings who have only the body without the soul? But what happened to the soul of the perpetrators of Holocaust when they were annihilating the bodies of their victims? If similar legacies of body torture remain in today's state legitimized forms, then can we interpret all our juridical and national programmes as the remnants of Auschwitz? The idea, Agamben argues, that the soul makes use of the body as an instrument and at the same time commands it, was formulated by Plato in his *Alcibiades* and Aristotle might have the soul-body relations in his mind while formulating the slave master relation. The soul seems to have much to do with the body. So keeping in mind the fact that the slave is the being whose work is "the use of body", he is not a human as Arsitotle defines *ergon* as the work or the proper function of the human being in his *Nicomachean Ethics*, something that the slave is denied or is excluded from

> It is necessary to add however that the special status of slaves—at once excluded from and included in humanity, as those not properly human beings who make it possible for others to be human—has as its consequence a cancellation and confounding of the limits that separates *physis* from *nomos*. Both artificial instrument and human being, the slave properly belongs neither to the sphere of nature nor that of convention, neither to the sphere of justice nor that of violence. Hence the apparent ambiguity of Aristotle's theory of slavery, which like ancient philosophy in general seems constrained to justify what it can only condemn and to condemn that of which it cannot deny the necessity. The fact is that the slave, although excluded from political life has an entirely special relation with it. The slave in fact represents a not properly human life that renders possible for others the *bios politicos*, that is to say, the truly human life. And if the human being is defined for the Greeks through a dialectic between *physis* and *nomos*, *zoe* and *bios*, then the slave like *bare life*, stands at the threshold that separates and joins them. (Agamben, 2016, 20)

The slave is then denied the *bios politicos*, or the truly human life and she/he is the one whose work consists only in the use of the body and hence there are some humans such as slaves who are less than humans, whose *ergon (the work or the proper function of the human being)*, Aristotle claims, is not human or is less than other humans. (Agamben, 2016, 5) This, as stated earlier, is crucial for my argumentative frame as human beings are subjected to the necessities of life, and they can be free only if they subject others, forcefully constraining them to endure those necessities for them (Agamben, 2016, 20). Our genealogical optic of human history would unveil how we have subjected different subaltern bodies for this purpose of meeting the necessities of the elite group of human family. The triadic category of the *convict-slave/subaltern-precariat* assumes greater relevance here as the large body of philosophic thought that endorsed the necessity of maintaining such bodily persecution of slaves and subalterns constituted all forms of subsequent ideas of state formation, nation building etc and today when we witness the defiling of bodies of minorities, migrants, Maoists, convicts, captives, etc we are actually continuing with similar classical tradition of *Homo Sacerization*. We may recall here Agamben's definition of the *Homo Sacer* as someone whom the Roman state used to declare as unworthy for sacrifice but whom ancient Roman law would exclude from its legal fold of protection and anyone can kill or torture the *Homo Sacer* without being charged with torture or murder. (Agamben, 1998)

Agamben correctly notes that the idea of *energeia (being at work)* and *chresis (use)*, have been juxtaposed in classical thinking and so have been the case with ideas of *psyche* and *soma*, soul and the body. Agamben's central question in his *The Use of Bodies* is, easy to grasp: What is ours, and how do we use it? Our body, for instance, is ours, as is the life we lead with it; but in what way, to what degree, subject to what restrictions? (Pozza, 2016) Agamben mentioned Foucault here who once said something quite significant about this. For Foucault, "historical research was like a shadow cast by the present onto the past. For him, this shadow stretched back to the 17th and 18th centuries but for Agamben the shadow is longer." (Pozza, 2016) Agamben's name for this depth of that deepest past which ontology, theology, philosophy, and poetry jointly explore—is "anthropogenesis."(Pozza, 2016) Talking about such past legacies, can we apply such vision of anthropogenesis to interpret present-day crimes of body subjections in the name of religion, nationalism, governance and militarization? Do we see the continuous biopolitical shadows of the past in such contemporary events of bloody norms? In the subsequent section I will engage with these questions in detail.

Dismembering the Other: The *Musselmann*, Corpses and the *Remnants of Auschwitz*

Agamben discussed in detail the figure of the *Musselmann* (the guards of the concentration camps who helped in the execution of Holocaust crimes) in his *Remnants of Auschwitz*

(1999) and I would argue that this figure continues to survive today in contemporary execution of state policies and state repression of citizens` bodies. For Agamben, the *Musselmann* is a limit concept. S/he is where dichotomies between man and non-man, dignity and non-dignity, human and inhuman, death and life collapse. Through them the true nature of the relationship between modern power and genocidal will, subjection and subjectivity are revealed. On the basis of his reading of numerous archival testimonies, Agamben shows that the *Musselmann* is the one who survives his humanity as he is dehumanized through hunger and pain yet goes on living, showing an inhuman capacity to suffer. He has no sociality while alive and therefore no dignity when killed: "In Auschwitz, people did not die; rather, corpses were produced" (Agamben, 1999, 71).This state that Agamben defines as the real horror of Auschwitz is accomplished because, in "Hitler's Germany, an unprecedented absolutizaton of the biopower to *make live* intersects with an equally absolute generalization of the sovereign power to *make die*, such that biopolitics coincide immediately with thanatopolitics" (Agamben, 1999, 83). This thanatopolitics of Auschwitz continues in regimes of biopower in our times whose objective is to produce, in a human body, the "absolute separation of the living being and the speaking being, zoë and bios, the inhuman and the human-survival" (Agamben, 1999, 156).Can there be a better philosophization on bodies or bare life? The categorical triad of *convict-slave/ subaltern-precariat* merely survives and is denied the proper living of a human in the name of civilization and juridical normativity and hence when a mob lynches an old Muslim in India for his alleged eating of beef, a habit not sanctioned by the reigning juridical norms, he is reduced to a mere bare life by the state so that anyone can kill the homo sacerized life of the old Muslim man with impunity in the name of national or religious identity.

So when the body of Mohammad Akhlaq Saifi was being lynched by a religious fanatic group in India in 2016 for his alleged consumption of beef, which is banned in Uttar Pradesh, India or when a body of a Dalit is burnt or dismembered by the upper caste rage in caste ridden states of India, the eyes of Kashmiri youths are penetrated by army pallet gun bullets, or the bodies of killed Maoist cadres are carried on bamboo poles like hunted animals, or the corpses of the hanged convict killed through death penalty are silently buried inside a high security prison, what do they augur about the body politic of a nation? All thoughts of the body actually transcend the body and there is the rub. For the state or for any institute of power, subsumption of the body of the deviant *other* or the docile follower assumes a crucial part of state policy for maintenance of power and seen through that angle bodies seem to trigger a lot to mind about and mind into. To borrow Foucault one may reiterate that there is an "elegance of the discipline" of nationalism that demands docile bodies of knowledge and a technology of subservient minds that lay down their bodies for the abstract machine called nation and that justifies the dismemberment of other bodies that defies the logic of all forms of disciplinary ideologies.

Punitive Measures and the Political Economy of Body Persecutions

The body therefore emerges as central to our understanding of history and the mechanisms of modern power and in this respect I go back to what Foucault said about the soul and the body in his analysis of power. The soul he said, is "the effect and instrument of a political anatomy, the soul is the prison of the body." (Foucault, 1991, 65) This is a remarkable way of looking into the technologies of disciplinary ideologies (soul) to which modern power subjects the body of the subaltern and the precariat. Mahasweta Devi has shown this in her poignant rendition of her gendered subalterns such as Joshoda and Gangor in her *Breast Stories*. Derrida has focused on the same in his analysis of death penalty but I will return on both these analytical illustrations in the subsequent sections. As of now

I will focus on Foucault's unpacking of the nexus between power and technologies of punitive measures or bodily persecutions.

Reading Foucault, we realize the fallacy of our traditional notion that the body obeys only the necessary and inherent laws of physiology and hence historic forces or cultures have no role to play on it. In reality however, "bodies are shaped by society" or to rephrase it, bodies too have a history. Foucault brought the body into focus by locating it in history and by connecting it with the "deployments of power". In short Foucault tried to study the metamorphosis of punitive methods on the basis of a political technology of the body and he discussed in his *Discipline and Punish* the linkages of different systems of punishment with the systems of production within which they operate—thus in a slave economy, punitive mechanisms serve to provide an additional labor force—and to constitute a body of civil slaves in addition to those provided by war or trading; with feudalism, at a time when money and production were still at an early stage of development, we find a sudden increase in corporal punishments—the body being in most cases the only property accessible; the penitentiary, forced labor, and the prison factory appear with the development of the mercantile economy. (Foucault, 1991, 67) So we can surely accept the general proposition that in our societies the systems of punishment are to be situated in a certain political economy of the body—even if they do not make use of violent or bloody mode of torture, even when they use "lenient" methods involving confinement or correction, it is always the body that is at issue—the body and its forces, their utility and their docility, their distribution and their submission. (Foucault, 1991, 68)

> The body is also directly involved in a political field; power relations have an immediate hold upon it, they invest it, mark it, train it, torture it, force it to carry our tasks, to perform ceremonies, to emit signs. This political investment of the body is bound up, in accordance with complex reciprocal relations,

> with its economic use, it is largely as a force of production that the body is invested with relations of power and domination, but, on the other hand its constitution as labor power is possible only if it is caught up in a system of subjection, ... the body becomes a useful force only if it is both a productive body and a subjected body. This subjection is not only obtained by the instruments of violence or ideology; it can also be direct, physical, pitting force against force, bearing on material elements, and yet without involving violence, it may be calculated, organized, technically thought out, it may be subtle, make use neither of weapons nor of terror and yet remain of a physical order. That is to say there may be a knowledge of the body that is not exactly the science of its functioning and a mastery of its forces that is more than the ability to conquer them: this knowledge and this mastery constitute what might be called the political technology of the body. Such technologies cannot be localized in a particular type of institution or state apparatus. What these apparatuses and institutions operate is a microphysics of power. The study of this microphysics presupposes that the power exercised on the body is conceived not as a property, but as a strategy. (Foucault, 1999, 26)

To analyse the political investment of the body and the microphysics of power presupposes the body politic as a set of material elements and techniques that serve as weapons. We have to situate the techniques of punishment- whether they seize the body in the ritual of public torture and execution or whether they are oriented towards the soul—in the history of this body politic; and if we do that then penal practices emerge less as a consequence of legal theories than as a part of political anatomy.

Our non-corporal soul, Foucault says, is not a substance, it is the element in which are articulated the effects of a certain type of power and the reference of a certain type of knowledge, the machinery by which the power relations give rise to a possible corpus of knowledge. In what follows we would see how such a corpus of knowledge leads to our legitimization of the killing or body tortures of the *convict-slave/subaltern-*

precariat. I will begin with Mahasweta Devi's "Breast Stories" to narrate the assault on the bodies of the gendered subalterns and then finally we would engage with Derrida's treatise on the death penalty and the dead body of the hanged convict.

Gendered Body as Parabolic Sign: Mahasweta Devi and Her *Breast Stories*

> There is a non-issue behind the bodice, there is a rape of the people behind it, Upin would have known if he had wanted to, could have known. (Mahasweta Devi, 2016, 138)

When we encounter the quoted lines in Mahasweta Devi's "Behind the Bodice", the last story in her collection of stories known as the *Breast Stories* translated and critically discussed by Gayatri Chakrabarty Spivak, we realize that there is indeed no 'non-issue' behind the bodice and Upin the photographer-gazer of female breasts in that story who represents all of us, should have realized that. In that way the *Breast Stories* and their critical enunciation by Spivak yield a lot for our project of reading the political economy of body and the conceptual triad of the *convict-slave/subaltern-precariat*. Spivak in her brilliant analysis of these stories has unraveled the politics of usurpation of the subaltern through the allegorical (she calls it parabolic) use of the breast. Here the breast "becomes a concept metaphor (rather than a symbol) of police violence in the democratic state". (Spivak, 2016, x) In Mahasweta's *Breast Stories*, as Spivak rightly points out, the "breast is not a symbol ... In *Draupadi*, what is represented is an erotic object transformed into an object of torture and revenge where the lines between heterosexuality and gender violence seems to waver." (Spivak, 2016, ix) In the story *Breast-Giver*, the breast is presented as "a survival object transformed into a commodity, making visible the indeterminacy between filial piety and gender violence..." (Spivak, 2016, x) In a similar vein, in the story, *Behind the Bodice*, Mahasweta bitterly decries the supposed normality of sexuality as male violence.

Interestingly enough, Mahasweta Devi's own account was

that the story *Stannadyani* (Breast Giver) is a parable of India after decolonization. She believes that like the protagonist Jashoda in that story, India is a mother-by-hire. All classes of people who are sworn to "protect the new state, abuse and exploit her" and as long as there is this hegemonic cultural self-representation of India as a goddess-mother (dissimulating the possibility that this mother is a slave), she will collapse under the burden of the immense expectations that such a self-representation permits. (Spivak, 2016, 72) Mahasweta's text, in this context, also show in many ways how the "narrative of nationalism have been and remain irrelevant to the life of the subordinate. The elite culture of nationalism participated and participates with the colonizer in various ways." (Spivak, 2016, 74) We need to revisit incidents of Dalit killing and lynching of Muslims in India in the light of the above statement as for poor Dalits and poor Muslims like Mohammad Akhlaq, nationalism is a word that they are compelled to learn through the elite system of body coercions.

Spivak reads Mahasweta's stories as typifying the "subaltern as the gendered subject" that goes against the allegorical theme of Mother India. When in the name of *Bharat Mata* we spawn the ideologies of a virulent and rabid form of ultra-nationalism, we are actually forgetting the inherent contradiction of gendered subalternization as well as nationalist subalternization. I would argue that Jasodha the *Stanadayani* who works as a milk-mother in her owner's house, feeding the owner's grandsons through her surplus milk, is not only a gendered subaltern as described by Spivak but she is also a nationalist-subaltern who has to bear the burden of a national religious metaphor of a breast giving, caring foster mother named after the mythological foster mother of Lord Krishna. Here Jashoda's act of surplus feeding is projected as pure body exploitation and both Mahasweta and Spivak also foregrounds the religious and nationalist nature of such exploitation as throughout that story the religious overtone of maternal benevolence is heightened to silence the real act of body coercion. The fact that ultimately Jashoda died of breast cancer because of the overuse of her body is also significant in making her a nationalist subaltern because as the republic kills her own children in the name of nationalism, Jashoda is killed in the name of motherly benevolence that has a nationalist ring. In the story *Draupadi*, which is the first story in the *Breast Stories*, Dopdi Mejhen, the tribal Naxalite too is brutally raped and bodily mutilated in the police station in the name of nation and national security. In her reading, Spivak however also sees the subaltern as the subject of her own history and in a Marxist Feminist reading of *Breast Giver*, she reminds us that one of the fallacies of Marxist labor theory of value is that it does not take sexual reproduction into account when speaking of social reproduction or the reproduction of labor power. The political economy or the sexual division of labour changes considerably by the sale of Jashoda's labor power which is unique to her female reproductive use value. According to Spivak, the emergence of (exchange) value and its immediate appropriation in *Stanadayini* may be thematized in the following way

> The milk that is produced in one's own body for one's children is a use value. When there is a superfluity of use values, exchange values arise. That which cannot be used is exchanged. As soon as the exchange value of Jasodha's milk emerges, it is appropriated. Good food and constant sexual servicing are provided so that she can be kept in the prime condition of optimum lactation. The milk she produces for her children is presumably through necessary labor. The milk that she produces for the children of her master's family is surplus labor. (Spivak, 2016, 79-80)

This parabolic or allegorical reading cannot be disqualified by the fact that Jasoda's body produces a surplus that is fully consumed by the owners of her labor power. Here Spivak poses the following question,

> Am I then proposing to endorse some weird theory where labor power is replaced by the power of gestation and lactation? Or am I suggesting that the study of this particular female activity,

> professional mothering, as it is to be found... be included in any study of the subaltern? (Spivak, 2016, 81)

Knowing that her breasts are the bread winners, Jasodha has to constantly keep them filled with milk. Spivak again observes, "Just as the wage worker cannot distinguish between necessary and surplus labor, so the gendered proletarian- serving the *oikos* rather than the *polis* with nothing but her (power to produce) offspring—comes to call the so called sanctity of motherhood into question." (Spivak, 2016, 83)

The Marxian hypothesis of labor is expanded by Spivak to include the lactating mother who produces a use-value. But for whose use are we talking about? Even if we read "the story as a proto-nationalist parable about Mother India, it is the failure of this exchange that is the substance of the story. (Spivak, 2016, 85) Having located the story in the nationalist narrative of colonization and decolonization, Spivak made these superb observations

> ... In the theatres of decolonization, the relationships between indigenous and imperialist systems of domination are also dialectical... [talking about the economic sphere] that sphere is the site of the production of value, not things. As I have mentioned earlier, it is the body's susceptibility to the production of value which makes it vulnerable to idealization and therefore to insertion into the economic. This is the ground of the labor theory of value. It is here that the story of the emergence of value from Jashoda's labor power infiltrates Marxism and questions its gender specific presuppositions. The production of people through sexual reproduction and affective socialization. (Spivak, 2016, 86)

So the body's susceptibility to the production of values makes it vulnerable to both idealization and greater subalternization and this is proved not just in the case of the *Breast Giver* but also in case of Draupadi (in *Draupadi*) and Gangor (in *Behind the Bodice*). Gangor's breasts are projected as a national erotic emblem where the popular Hindi movie song *choli ke pichhe keya hai (what is there behind the bodice?)* almost becomes, according to Mahasweta, a virtual national anthem across India at that time. So the susceptibility of the breast to yield to values as a parabolic sign leads to its cooptation. Dopdi Mejhen, the Naxalite woman in the story *Draupadi* is not just ideologically killed but is also physically mutilated in the police station by the ideological state apparatus of the Indian state. Mahasweta's gendered subalterns such as Jashoda, Draupadi, and Gangor also expand the thematic of the "woman's political body." This leads us to my final engagement with the politics of the body and in my view the fullest and clearest form of this legitimized politics of the body is evident in the rule of death penalty which has also been justified in India and in many other countries in the name of national interest. It would not be incorrect to suggest that so far in the previous sections we have been actually deliberating in various forms of capital punishments. The *Homo Sacer* is nothing but a legally ordained non-legalized death penalty convict and when we subject the convict or the subaltern like Draupadi to incredible body brutalization we are actually witnessing the universal shadow of the death penalty and the legacy of Auschwitz continuing through varied instances of capital punishment. I would therefore, argue that any excursus on minding the body must conclude with a genealogical study of the death penalty as done by Derrida and in what follows I would see how the biggest form of politics with the body is done through the highest form of punitive measures—legalized murders. This can happen within the prison or outside the prison through false encounters, mob lynching, social exclusions, etc.

The Body of the Condemned and Death Penalty

Walter Benjamin's observation that "all violence as a means is either law-making or law-preserving" (Benjamin, 1996, 243) and in a similar vein, Derrida's distinction between "law, which is always complicit with violence and always susceptible to deconstruction, and justice, which is not deconstructible" (Derrida, 1992, 15) underscore the closure/

cruelty at the heart of law. For Derrida, "deconstruction takes place in the interval that separates the undeconstructibility of justice from the deconstructibility of *droit* [French for law and right] (authority, legitimacy, and so on). It is possible as an experience of the impossible, there where, even it does not exist (or does not yet exist, or never does exist), *there is* justice."(ibid) Let us inquire then, what remains after the body of the lawless/Beast is (un)lawfully executed, or the D/evil is bodily terminated. What awaits the burial of the dead or the cremation of the executed corpse? Can we imagine what it takes to be a corpse? Once the terminable/already terminated signifier is taken off the syntactic order of law by law, what are the remnants?—bloody froth coming out of the mouth, mangled/deformed physiognomy, protruding eyes or jutting out tongues, swollen neck, or a charred electrocuted viscera? The executed law-breaker becomes a corpse after execution and is given a human treatment after the termination is over, but do we allow that human status to the *Homo Sacer* before it becomes the corpse? *Hominess sacri* has to die to regain its human status, in other words, corpse as a signifier is accorded a differential logic and death penalty assumes the role of *writing* where execution is infinitely deferred because every time we execute a criminal (state-defined), his criminality is erased and humanity restored. So capital punishment punishes the criminal to anoint him again as a human being, and herein resides the aporetic/aleatory character of such a legal device. Let us get back then to the original question, what remains after the execution?—The surplus of death?, the non-incorporable *absence-presence* of the convict?, the invisible visibility of the criminal, or a perpetual rise in crimes? Is purgation/social cleansing complete after the guillotine falls? Or, what remains are, the satisfaction of the judiciary, the relief of the Sovereign, the relaxation of the prison authorities, the celebration of society or the remainder/excess/surplus/specter of the convict? This question haunts and the hauntology of capital punishment has definitely got a philosophic undercurrent. To philosophize is to engage with death, in other words, to die is to invite philosophy to unfurl its limits anew, but what about executions? To execute is to arrive at a fore-closure or to open the flood gates of philosophy? The dead body of Afzal Guru, the Indian terrorist who was hanged to death in February, 2013, was not handed over to his family members and his body was buried in the prison premises after the hanging. His wife was informed about his hanging after the execution was over and his son was denied a last meeting with his accused father. No explanations were given about this state of exception. The Sovereign knows and the rest is silence. Death penalty is a drug/sedative and sometimes a tranquilizer or entertainer (there were celebrations in different parts of India after Afzal's hanging) that normalizes/anaesthetizes state killing in the name of law (Kamuf, 2012). The hemlockization of Socrates was also attended, Derrida reminds us, with similar silences or celebrations, but then from the interstices of silent addiction/acceptance erupts a new economy of subjectivity. How would philosophy react to such events of sovereign exception? Should Afzal have been buried at all or thrown into the gutter after the execution, a beast best left away to be devoured by real beasts? But then the 'animal that we are', has a different logic and we normally accord human treatment to the executed corpse. But why do we bridge the ontic with the ontological here? Why do we humanize after complete beastification? In the bio-political continuum, where the Auschwitz legacy continues in sovereign penology within the four walls of the modern prison, what are the dividing lines between state killing and barbarity? In other words, why and how do we package the gruesome as the normative? How does hanging, electrocution, custodial torture, beheading get robed in the divine or the normative? Philosophy has its task cut out on this body politics of the divine and Derrida has rightly addressed these theologico-political questions in his Death Penalty seminar published in English translation in 2014. In the next concluding section I will elaborate on this to arrive at a conclusion of our discussion on minding the body.

Conclusion: Dismemberment of Bodies and the Festival of Cruelty

Rousseau, Locke, Hobbes and Kant, all, in spite of being philosophical stalwarts, Derrida complains, endorsed the idea of death penalty. Derrida in his book, *Death Penalty* (2014) severely takes Kant to task for his juridical categorical imperatives which Derrida through his Nietzschean study of Kant, says, smacks of cruelty/are soaked in blood. Rousseau's *The Social Contract* too justifies the death penalty where in Chapter 5 of Book 2, titled, "On the Right of Life and Death", Rousseau posits the outrageous logic that

> the citizen receives his life from the state, and therefore has no right over his life ... life is no longer merely a bounty of nature, but a conditional gift of the state ... Insurance contract: if you want your life to be protected, then you must accept that if you kill, you will be killed." (Derrida, 14-15)

Derrida's primary objective in his book on Death Penalty is to investigate the genealogy of capital punishment and to do that he began by probing into the trials and subsequent execution of four iconic figures, namely—Socrates, Jesus, Hallaj and Joan of Arc—all of whom were accused of blasphemy and religious incriminations and if closely studied it becomes evident that the theologico-political power of the sovereign state is deeply inscribed in the history of the death penalty. Given that, the philosophic task of deconstruction, according to Derrida should be to unpack the genealogy of death penalty

> If one wants to ask oneself "What is the death penalty?" or "What is the essence and meaning of the death penalty?" it will indeed be necessary to reconstitute this history and this horizon of sovereignty as the hyphen in the theologico-political. An enormous history, the whole history that at the moment we are only touching on or glimpsing. It is not even certain that the concept of history and the concept of horizon resist a deconstruction of the scaffolding of these scaffolds ... History the

> concept of history is perhaps linked, in its very possibility, in its scaffolding, to the Abrahamic and above all the Christian history of sovereignty, and thus of the possibility of the death penalty as theologico-political violence. Decosntrcution is perhaps always, ultimately, through the deconstruction of carno-phallogocentrism, the deconstruction of this historical scaffolding of the death penalty, of the history of this scaffold. Deconstruction, what is called by that name, is perhaps, perhaps the deconstruction of the death penalty, of the logocentric, logonomocentric scaffolding in which the death penalty is inscribed and prescribed. (Derrida, 2014, 22-23)

But what is the theologico-political? And the answer Derrida gives is also revealing –

> The theologico-political is a system, an apparatus of sovereignty in which the death penalty is necessarily inscribed. There is theologico-political wherever there is death penalty. (Derrida, 2014, 23)

Having finished the first session, Derrida now moves to the subsequent one and dwells on Foucault's analysis of the history of punishment where he spoke about the phenomenon of the spectacle associated with the death penalty. Foucault's observation about the de-spectacularisation of the death penalty with the arrival of the guillotine in the early 19th century is taken up by Derrida later in the book where he elaborately engages on the guillotine as discussed by Camus and others. Foucault's horrific examples of barbaric tortures in the name of punishment during 16th and 17th centuries and the piercing cry of the tortured convict for pardon brings in the issue of pardon which Derrida describes as "beyond the structure of law", and hence the common perception that the pardon of a heinous crime must be exceptional. But Derrida would begin his lecture session of December 15 as contained in his book on Death Penalty exactly with this question, "what is an exception?" A pardon, Derrida observes, is always "outside the law, always heterogeneous to order, to norm, to rule, or to calculation ... to economic as well as juridical calculation."

(Derrida, 2014, 47)

I will conclude this discussion with this ring of the "outside the law" because if the body is to be minded it has to be addressed in the light of our discussion of the theologico-political sovereignty that assigns a control over the sovereign over the body of the *convict-subaltern-precariat*. We may call this control over bodies, thanatopolitics, Auschwitz legacy or the remnants of the concentration camp and the *constituted power* of such sovereign command can only be reversed through the *constituent potential* of the bare body of the *homo sacer* or the slave-subaltern-precariat. This simultaneous vulnerability and resistant potentiality of the bare life (body) of the *homo sacer*, in our analysis, is the best subject to focus on any project of minding the body. Dopdi Mejhen in the penultimate part of the story *Draupadi* in Mahasweta Devi's *Breast Stories*, menacingly teased the police officer, who brutally gender assaulted her the previous night inside the prison to repeat the same gruesome assault. She refused to put on any clothes (she was disrobed the previous night by the police brutality) and her bare bodied bloody outcry in that custodial scene, to our mind, best exemplifies the *constituent potential* that can deconstruct the *constituted* command of the sovereign over the body of the precariat.

REFERENCES

Agamben, Giorgio, *The Use of Bodies, Homo Sacer IV, 2*, Translated by Adam Kotsko, Stanford, California: Satnford University Press, 2016.

Agamben, Giorgio, Homo Sacer, Sovereign Power and Bare Life, Translated by Daniel Heller-Roazen, Stanford, California: Stanford University Press, 1998.

Agamben, Giorgio, *Remnants of Auschwitz: The Witness and the Archive*, New York: Zone Books, 2002.

Crane, Tim and Sarah Patterson, *History of the Mind Body Problem*, London and New York: Routledge, 2002.

Devi, Mahasweta, *Breast Stories*, Translated by Gayatri Chakravorty Spivak, Kolkata: Seagull Books, 2016.

Derrida, Jacques. *The Gift of Death*, Trans. David Wills, Chicago: University of Chicago Press, 1992.

Derrida, Jacques, *The Death Penalty*, Vol. eds. Geoffrey Bennington, Marc Crepon, and Thomas Dutoit, Translated by Peggy Kamuf, Chicago & London: The University of Chicago Press, 2014.

Foucault, Michel, *History of Sexuality*, Vol. 1, An Introduction, trans. Robert Hurley, New York: Random House, 1978.

Guillaume Laura and Joe Hughes, ed., *Deleuze and the Body*, Edinburgh: Edinburgh University Press, 2011.

Kamuf, P., "Protocol: Death Penalty Addiction", *The Southern Journal of Philosophy*, Vol. 50, Spindel Supplement, 2012.

Merquior, J. G., *Foucault*, Great Britain: Fontana Press, 1985.

Mills, Sara, *Michel Foucault*, London and New York: Routledge, 2007.

Pozza, Neri, Review of *L'uso dei corpi. Homo sacer, IV, 2*, Giorgio Agamben, *Boston Reviews*, January 26, 2016, available at http://bostonreview.net/books-ideas/de-la-durantaye-agamben

Standing, Guy, *The Precariat: The New Dangerous Class*, London: Bloomsbury, 2014.

Rabinow, Paul, ed. *The Foucault Reader, An Introduction to Foucault's Thought*, London: Penguin Books, 1991.

Taylor, Dianna, ed., *Michel Foucault: Key Concepts*, Acumen Publication, Durham, 2011.

4

Hangman's Metaphysics and Penology-to-come: Provincializing Derrida's Death Penalty Seminar

The [terrorist] incident, which resulted in heavy casualties, had shaken the entire nation and the collective conscience of the society will only be satisfied if the capital punishment is awarded to the offender. The challenge to the unity, integrity and sovereignty of India by these acts of terrorists and conspirators, can only be compensated by giving the maximum punishment to the person who is proved to be the conspirator in this treacherous act. The appellant, who is a surrendered militant and who was bent upon repeating the acts of treason against the nation, is a menace to the society and his life should become extinct. Accordingly, we uphold the death sentence."

—Indian Supreme Court Judgment on August 4, 2005 for the execution of Afzal Guru, the terrorist, Execution was carried out on Ninth February, 2013.

An eye for an eye will make the whole world blind.

—Mahatma Gandhi

Forgiveness forgives only the unforgivable.

—Derrida, 2001, 32

A decision that didn`t go through the ordeal of the undecidable would not be a free decision, it would only be the programmable application or unfolding of a calculable process. It might be legal; it would not be just. (Derrida, 1994, 24)

Indeed these killers are Brahma *(God); these servants (or slaves) are* Brahma*; these cheats and rogues are also manifestation of*

> *one and the same* Brahma *itself.*
>
> —*Brahmasukta* of *Atharvaveda*

> *No philosophy against the death penalty.*
>
> —Derrida (*Death Penalty 1*, 24).

> *We should be certainly engaging deconstruction in a new materialism.* —Catherine Malabou, 2009, 61

Let us begin here in this chapter with exploring the possibility of impossibilities, with the encrypton of the irruptive economy of singularities, with an ethics of *dharma*/responsibility that envisages the *a venir*, dislodging given *a priories* like the Kantian law of Talion or the categorical imperative of *Rechtslehre*, or the doctrine of right (Bennington, 2012, 23). Is non-violence the real divine violence that substitutes all mythical/state violence? In other words, is *ahimsa* (non-violence) the real *plasticity* of philosophy-to-come? Walter Benjamin's observation that "all violence as a means is either law-making or law-preserving" (Benjamin, 1996, 243)and in a similar vein, Derrida's distinction between 'law, which is always complicit with violence and always susceptible to deconstruction, and justice, which is not deconstructible' (Derrida, 1992, 15) underscore the closure/ cruelty at the heart of law. For Derrida, "deconstruction takes place in the interval that separates the undeconstructibility of justice from the deconstructibility of *droit* [French for law and right] (authority, legitimacy, and so on). It is possible as an experience of the impossible, there where, even it does not exist (or does not yet exist, or never does exist), *there is* justice." (ibid) Anachronies, said Derrida, make laws (Derrida, 1994, 7) and in a world of disjointed temporalities, where time is interminably out of joint, the *non-time*, or the Blanchot's *non-origin* belies (Haase and Large, 2001, 51-66) any possibility of a synchrony and therefore, traversing the solidities of the Real, navigating from the ontic to the ontological, one encounters frequent transgressions of law and consequent sate inflicted death or death sentences that appear as bizarre imperative sentences whose syntactical tautness inflicts a different grammar of bare life or self-negating ontology that dislodges Heidegger's *Being-towards-death* with a *Dasein-towards-the-gallows*. But what remains after the body of the lawless/Beast is (un)lawfully executed, or the D/evil is bodily terminated? What awaits the burial of the dead or the cremation of the executed corpse? Can we imagine what it takes to be a corpse? Once the terminable/already terminated signifier is taken off the syntactic order of law by law, what are the remnants?—bloody froth coming out of the mouth, mangled/deformed physiognomy, protruding eyes or jutting out tongues, swollen neck, or a charred electrocuted viscera? The executed law-breaker becomes a corpse after execution and is given a human treatment after the termination is over, but do we allow that human status to the *Homo Sacer* before it becomes the corpse? *Hominess sacri* has to die to regain its human status, in other words, the corpse as a signifier is accorded a differential logic and death penalty assumes the role of *writing* where execution is infinitely deferred because every time we execute a criminal (state-defined), his criminality is erased and humanity restored. So capital punishment punishes the criminal to anoint him again as a human being, and herein resides the aporetic/aleatory character of such a legal device. Let us get back then to the original question, what remains after the execution?—The surplus of death?, the non-incorporable *absence-presence* of the convict?, the invisible visibility of the criminal, or a perpetual rise in crimes? Is purgation/social cleansing complete after the guillotine falls? Or, what remains are, the satisfaction of the judiciary, the relief of the Sovereign, the relaxation of the prison authorities, the celebration of society or the remainder/excess/surplus/specter of the convict? This question haunts and the hauntology of capital punishment has definitely got a philosophic undercurrent. To philosophize is to engage with death, in other words, to die is to invite philosophy to unfurl its limits anew, but what about executions? To execute is to arrive at a fore-closure or to open the flood gates of philosophy? The dead body of Afzal Guru, the Indian terrorist who was hanged to death in February, 2013, was not handed over to his family members and his body was buried in the prison premises after the hanging. His wife was informed about his hanging after the execution was over and his son was denied a last meeting with his accused father. No explanations were given about this state of exception. The Sovereign knows and the rest is silence. Death penalty is a drug/sedative and sometimes a tranquilizer or entertainer (there were celebrations in different parts of India after Afzal's hanging) that normalizes/anaesthetizes state killing in the name of law (Kamuf, 2012). The hemlockization of Socrates was also attended, Derrida reminds us, with similar silences or celebrations, but then from the interstices of silent addiction/acceptance erupts a new economy of subjectivity. How would philosophy react to such events of sovereign exception? Should Afzal have been buried at all or thrown into the gutter after the execution, a beast best left away to be devoured by real beasts? But then the 'animal that we are, has a different logic and we normally accord human treatment to the executed corpse. But why do we bridge the ontic with the ontological here? Why do we humanize after complete beastification? In the bio-political continuum, where Auschwitzion continues sovereign penology in the four walls of the modern prison, what are the dividing lines between state killing and barbarity? In other words, why and how do we package the gruesome as the normative? How does hanging, electrocution, beheading get robed in the divine? Philosophy has its task cut out on this politics of the divine and Derrida has rightly addressed these theologico-political questions in his Death Penalty seminar to be published in English translation in October this year.

The enormous subsumption of western life and law by the Abrahamic theologico-political or the carno-phallogo-centric paradigms prompted Derrida to say that perhaps there was no death penalty outside Europe and deconstruction is 'deconstruction of the death penalty'. We definitely need to overlook Derrida's overstatement about the Euro-centric scope of death penalty, but drawing on Derrida's philosophic challenge to unveil the logic of death penalty, we argue that to restrict the death penalty debate only within the Abrahamic tradition would be a cognitive mistake as Indian philosophy engaged with capital punishment and penal cruelty thousands of years ago much ahead of Christianity. This provincialization of the death penalty debate would strengthen the logic of deconstruction and justice. The video footage of Saddam Hussein holding the noose himself, examining the tautness of the rope before his execution, the sight of Afghan President Abdullah being dragged by the Taliban to be beaten and hanged to death in Kabul or Colonel Gaddafi being killed by the dissenting militia of Libya with the help of the American army or for that matter the killing of a criminal by a jubilant mob in broad day-light on the open street—in all these instances are inscribed a notion of finality, justification, culmination, satisfaction, erasure, abolition, annihilation, etc. But then to reiterate the same philosophic question, what remains after the bullet is fired, after the lynching, the tug at the rope, the switching of electrocution? The bloody lifeless body, or the surplus of death or the carcass of law? Capital punishment reinscribes the aporia of death and the ethics of life. The *absence-presence* of the executed convict, his/her trace or remainder allows us to deconstruct the very act of execution. The ontology of execution is always already challenged as the remainder remains in the form of mourning, anger, or introspection or in the spectrality of the event. The eruption of justice from the scaffold of blood is marred by the legacy of hauntology. Is death penalty a gift of the judicial system? A gift to mankind or has mankind invented such a gift for justice? But then Derrida would talk of a different gift of death, as did Jainism and the *Upanishads*, the Indian philosophical texts thousands of years earlier, a gift that entails a *dharma* or care for responsibility which calls for violence without violence or a law beyond law, that is justice. The present essay seeks to thematize the onto-thanato-politics or *gallows-sovereign-politics* of capital punishment in the light of Derrida's Death Penalty Seminars and Giorgio Agamben's notions of the *Homo Sacer* and *Bare life*. In the process, it attempts an epoche of the whole death penalty debate to arrive at a possible emanation of a new grammar of Being in the coming community premised on the scaffold of forgiveness, love, justice and the *Brahman* (supreme attachment for all). Harold Coward in his fascinating work, *Derrida and Indian Philosophy* (1990) examined the close associations between Derridean Deconstruction and Indian philosophy and in the present article, emboldened by Coward's pioneering scholarly enterprise, we venture to intervene in Derrida's Death Penalty Seminar debate from a *Vedantist or Advaidist* philosophical parallax view. What prompted us to engage Derrida with the axio-noetic gnosis of Indian philosophy is the former's disdain over Western philosophy's silence on the question of death penalty. The execution of Socrates was attended by a Hemlock society of philosophers (if we may say so) whose philosophic dumbness later culminated in the justification of capital punishment by stalwarts like Plato, Kant and Hegel. The Hangman's metaphysics gradually gained ground and became a norm. Derrida's discomfort over Western philosophical advocacy of death penalty and its theologico-political genealogy is understandable and what constitutes the central argument in his death penalty seminar is a philosophical nemesis, a philosophical abolitionist doctrine that negates the logics of capital punishment philosophically instead of pursuing abolition through Christian abstractionism. Derrida, we argue, would have taken heart from the fact that Indian philosophy engaged with this issue of capital/absolute punishment and its attended question of sovereign right or discretion much before Socrates was put to death. The Indian philosophico-epical text, *Mahabharata*, written nearly three thousand years ago focused on the question of righteousness and punishment and in what follows we would engage with Indian philosophy to demonstrate how it addressed this issue. Derrida's impatience with Western philosophy for its pro-cruelty stance and his subsequent dream for a truly philosophical analysis of death penalty can materialize through a study of *Vedantism, Advaitism and* the basic tenets of Buddhism and Jaina philosophy. In the subsequent section I will show how Derridean interpretation of ethics coalesces with the *Vedantist* idea of *Brahman* and *Dharma.*

Mysterium Tremendum, Brahman and the Ethics of Responsibility

Derrida relates responsibility (ethics/morality) to secrecy or to the mystery of the sacred, the *mysterium tremendum* through an analysis of the Czech philosopher Jan Patocka's *Heretical Essays on the Philosophy of History* in his *The Gift of Death* (Derrida, 1995). Patocka understands the development of the sense of the mysterious in terms of "orgiastic" religion which gave way to Platonism, which in turn gave way to Christianity. Patocka argues for the superiority of Christianity solely in terms of its understanding of the *mysterium tremendum*. Christianity's superiority is defined in terms of the universally accessible *tremendum*. From Patocka, Derrida gleans the understanding of the *mysterium tremendum* as that which, when encountered, produces the terrible (*tremendum*) realization that what is required (of us) is our entire Being. This sense of the *mysterium* rouses us to the responsibility of making a gift of our death, that is, of sacrificing one's self in the face of God (Sadler, 2004). Derrida believes that while responsibility and sacrifice are premised in the *mysterium tremendum,* they likewise ultimately transcend traditional ethics and morality. Such responsibility causes one to tremble (*tremendum*) in that it alludes to an unpredictable future, representing that to which one is drawn and yet which cannot be fulfilled without the loss of oneself. Here Derrida turns to Kierkegaard's *Fear and Trembling* as an exposition of such dread in the face of the unknown. Derrida envisages a coming community and

> the smooth functioning of such a society, the monotonous complacency of its discourses on morality, politics, and the law, and the exercise of its rights, are in no way impaired by the fact that, because of the structure of the laws of the market that society has instituted and controls, because of the mechanisms of external debt and other similar inequities, that same "society" puts to death or allows to die of hunger and disease tens of millions of children without any moral or legal tribunal ever being considered competent to judge such a sacrifice, the sacrifice of others to avoid being sacrificed oneself. (86)

Once such a structure of conscience exists, then Derrida proposes an understanding of God as "the name of the possibility I have of keeping a secret that is visible from the interior but not from the exterior". (109) Here Derrida replaces the traditional notion of God with the incorporeal, radically individualistic element of personal existence, and in so doing likewise transfers the origin of responsibility from a dreadful encounter with the transcendent *mysterium* to an indiscernible (secret) encounter with the invisible within oneself (Sadler, 2004). This is identical with the idea of *Dharma* or the ethics of responsibility as enunciated in the Vedanta and the *Upanishads*. This sense of the Being negates any law of the logos and in *The Specters of Marx*, Derrida characterizes the project of deconstruction as a political one and he envisages its task as,

> "[N]amely the deconstruction of the 'proper', of logocentrism, linguisticism, phonologism, the demystification or the de-sedimentation of the autonomic hegemony of language (a deconstruction in the course of which is elaborated another concept of the text or the trace, of their originary technization, of iterability, of the prosthetic supplement, but also of the proper and what was given the name exappropriation.)" (1994, p. 93)

Deconstruction, also characterized as a textual and academic project of denaturalization, is inherently political for Derrida, not because it leads to direct political action through prescription, but because it leads to the possibility of action which can try to think itself as responsible action, precisely because the subject of this action questions the historically given, sedimented in language, conditions of its action and thought. In the subsequent section we would see that the *Upanishadic* idea of the *Brahman* too is premised on a deconstructive ethics of questioning the pre-given, opening the being for the Other or constituting the ethics of alterity and justice premised on equivalence. Levinas reminds us that responsibility is not at first responsibility of myself for myself, that the sameness of myself is derived from the other, as if it were second to the other, coming to itself as responsible and mortal from the position of my responsibility before the other, for the other's death and in the face of it. In the first place it is because the *other* is mortal that my responsibility is singular and "inalienable". (1995, p. 46)

> we must always start over... Each generation must begin again to reinvolve itself in it without counting on the generation before. It thus describes the nonhistory of absolute beginnings which are repeated, and the very historicity that presupposes a tradition to be reinvented every step of the way, in this incessant repetition of the absolute beginning. (1995, p. 80)

This non-history of absolute beginning characterizes the Death Penalty seminars and Indian philosophy typifies the same through its enunciation of *philosophia perennis*. The present cannot be the past or the future, nor can it be simply itself. And, it will never be any different, yet it will never be the same. The degree to which and the conditions under which the time is out of joint will never be the same. And, yet, even though the present, by being thought, by being questioned, is revealed as requiring a decision, on the basis of a relationship to alterity, to others who one realizes, must be approached, difficult as it is, as singularities, this present, the present of a subject who realizes that their present is anachronistic, that their singularity is already contaminated by irresponsibility, this present is the only place where there is still the possibility of redress: "no differ*a*nce without alterity, no alterity without singularity, no singularity without here-now" (1994, p. 31).

This philosophical urge for alterity and deconstruction would be better understood if we realize the theologico-political matrix behind the logic of death penalty and the following section would discuss Derrida's genealogical reading of death penalty.

Exposing the Theologico-Political

Death penalty, according to Derrida, reconfigures the nature of sovereignty in the prince's or the state's power over the life and death of its citizens (*DP1* 9). In as much as the death penalty is considered an exception to the right to life, it offers an exemplary access to Schmitt's claim, which Derrida looks at in Session three, that "Sovereign is he who decides on the exception" (*DP1* 106-108). Derrida demonstrates how every claim either *for* or *against* the death penalty borrows in some way from a theologico-political and from a Judeo-Christian heritage. This will help explain why the four cases Derrida chooses to examine (Socrates, Jesus, al-Hallaj, and Joan of Arc) are all cases of the death penalty being applied by a state against a religious claim or against a claim to another transcendence (Naas, 2012). In the same way, then, that the debate between critics and partisans of the death penalty opposes *not* a wholly secular, areligious, or anti-religious position to a Christian position but, as we will see, two different aspects of the Christianity, and Derrida's four cases feature *not* an opposition between state claims to transcendence and claims against transcendence in general but claims to a *counter*-transcendence that threatens the state. Derrida's claims about democracy, the animal, and the death penalty are all aimed at the very same "carno-phallogocentric" tradition that places man, and often a certain transcendence of man, at its center (Naas, 2012). Thus even when the death penalty is opposed by writers (such as Hugo), the opposition is formulated on the basis of an emphasis on *human* life (as opposed to animal life). To question the death penalty, then, is to question the "carno-phallogocentrism" of which a certain thinking of democracy, of literature, of man in relation to the animal, and of sovereignty all form an essential part (*DP1* 31). Derrida goes on to find in Hugo what he calls an ambiguous Christian axiomatics (*DP1* 133). While Hugo wants to put an end to the death penalty and to the conception of sovereignty it implies, he wishes to do so, Derrida underscores, through a *divine* means; as Derrida writes, "the abolitionist instrument must be divine" (*DP1* 135). Derrida concludes this part of his argument:

> Hugo's abolitionism is profoundly Christian, Christlike, evangelical. Whether it is a matter here of profound faith or of obligatory rhetoric or, as I believe, between the two, a matter of a moral conscience or of a discourse of moral conscience, of an *inner* conviction [*for intérieur*] that can be cultivated as an authority only in a Christian space, of an idea of man, of "human life," of the inviolability of life as human life that is fundamentally heir to and elementarily the offspring of a Christian family, a holy family, it remains that it is in the name of God and of a Christian God that the death penalty is going to be opposed. (*DP1* 135, Naas, 2012)

We can thus trace a line from ancient Athens and Jerusalem to the medieval God as sovereign ruler over creation, and then from the divine right of the king as God's representative on earth (as the Pope still is in the Vatican), to the democratic revolution that, despite beheading the king, replaces God with "the people" as an indivisible sovereign. Implicit in this historicist reading might be the objective to seek to finally shake off this onto-theological heritage so as to enter into a truly secular age (Fritsch, 2012). Derrida "has always pursued 'as far as possible the necessity of a hyper-atheological discourse'" (55; Derrida 2004, 165). In an exceptional situation, "when the state deems it is threatened in its existence, it has the right to subsist even if it does so by pushing back the limits of the law," *in extremis*, by putting to death those it declares its enemies (*DP1*, 3). Death penalty is for Derrida the "keystone" of a theologico-political matrix welded together (cf. Derrida 2004,

147–48). In response to the abolitionism that makes abolition dependent on "order, peace, and security," Derrida appears at a first glance to call for the principled "unconditional right to life" in order to avoid what he calls "a fundamental, structural hypocrisy of the abolitionist discourse in its present state" (*DP1*, 3, Fritsch, 2012). In *For What Tomorrow*, Derrida says:

> As long as an abolitionist discourse has not been elaborated and effectively accredited (and this has not yet been done) at the level of unconditional principles, beyond the problems of purpose, exemplarity, utility, and even the 'right to life', we will not be shielded from a return to the death penalty. . . . The history of this problem is immense and complex: how to abolish the death penalty in a way that is based on principle, that is universal and unconditional, and not because it has become not only cruel but useless, insufficiently exemplary? (2004, 137)

Derrida might see this as part of the autodeconstruction of modern legal systems that philosophy has yet to grasp, for he charges that "never has any philosophy *as such* contested the legitimacy of the death penalty" (Derrida 2004, 146) but the subsequent section would demonstrate how Indian philosophy contested death penalty much earlier.

Ahimsa (Non-Violence) and Advaita Philosophy

The *Rig Veda* (ca. 1200 BC), one of the seminal texts of Indian philosophy defines the *Brahman*, as a state of being, or an impersonal concept, and *Brahman* is that state which is when all subject/object distinctions are obliterated. *Brahman* is ultimately a name for the experience of the timeless plentitude of being (Deutsch, 1973, 9) and a closer analysis would reveal that *Vedanta* philosophy is aligned to deconstruction as it defines *Brahman*, the supreme sense of being in the *Brihadaranyaka Upanishad*, II, 3, 6 via the negative, as *Neti Neti* (not this, not this), (Deutsch, 1973, 11). According to the *Upanishads*, all determination is negation, (*Brahmasutrabhasya, II, 1, 6.*) and *Brahman* is a state of silent being, and at the same time also a dynamic becoming. *Brahman* is divine and the divine is *Brahman*. In rising to the best in us we rise to the Self in us, to *Brahman*, to God himself. Thus when the Sage in the *Upanishads* is pressed for a definition of God, he remains silent, meaning that God is silence. When asked again to express God in words, he says, *Neti, Neti,* (Not this, Not this), but when pressed further for a positive explanation, he utters the sublimely simple words, '*Tat Tvam Asi*'(Thou art That) (Mascaro, 1965, 12). The words of Christ were, 'I am the Door; by me if any man enter in, he shall be saved, and shall pass in and out', but it is not enough to have reached the door; we must be admitted and there is a price for admission. *Vedantist* philosophy would argue that 'he that would save his soul, let him lose it' and to reincarnate the *Brahman* or the greater being, the baser being is to be sacrificed. (Coomaraswamy, 2000, 351) *Vedantist and Advaita* Philosophy believe in the idea of one Supreme Spirit or the *Paramatnam*, that pervades everywhere, including in human beings and every creature, formless and everlasting (ibid). Ethics according to *Vedanta* and the *Upanishads* begins with an awareness that our life is not of ourselves alone and there is another, greater life enfolding and sustaining us. Religion as man's search for this greater self will not accept any creeds as final or any laws as perfect. It will be evolutionary, moving over onward. The witness to this spiritual view is borne not only by the great religious teachers and leaders of mankind, but by the ordinary man on the street, in whose inmost being the well of the spirit is set deep. In his "The Doctrine of the Sword", Gandhi says,

> I do believe that when there is only a choice between cowardice and violence, I would advise violence ... I believe that non-violence is infinitely superior to violence, forgiveness more manly than punishment. Ksambut virrasya bhusanam ... non-violence is the law of our species as violence is the law of the brute. The spirit lies dormant in the brute and he knows no law but that of physical might. The dignity of man requires obedience to a higher law, to the strength of the spirit. (Radhakrishnan, 2010, 56)

Vedanta philosophy holds human behaviour as most important and the idea of correct behaviour, of living properly, of social order, law and morality, is summed up in the concept of "*dharma*". Every human being is expected to follow the *dharma* to the best of their ability; that is, to perform their duties to their family, community and society as a whole. Ancient Indian civilization had a highly developed system of religious, civil and criminal law and The "*Dharmasasbras*" and "*Arthasastras*" are the most detailed commentaries on these laws. The *Dharmasasbras* describes many crimes and their punishments and calls for the death penalty, even for crimes not resulting in death of another human being. But there are aspects of Indian philosophy which can be invoked to prevent the use of the death penalty. First of all the *Mahabharata, the great philosophico-epical text* itself contains passages arguing against the use of the death penalty in all cases. It argues against the use of the death penalty in a dialogue between one King Dyumatsena and his son Prince Satyavan in Chapter two hundred and fifty seven of the *Santiparva* or the Chapter on Peace. In this scene a number of men had been brought out for execution at the command of the King and Prince Satyavan asks the King, "Sometimes virtue assumes the form of sin and sin assumes the form of virtue. It is not possible that the destruction of individuals can ever be virtuous". King Dyumatsena replies: "If the spring of those who should be killed be virtuous, if robbers be spared, Satyavan, all distinction between virtue and vice will disappear". Satyavan responds:

> Without destroying the body of the offender, the king should punish him as ordained by the scriptures. The king should not act otherwise, neglecting to reflect upon the character of the offence and upon the science of morality . . .The extermination of the wicked is not in consonance with the eternal law. (Vyasa, 580)

Similarly, *The Vedanta* notion of punishment is not based on revenge, rather, punishment in the Indian philosophical scheme should be aimed at restoring the proper social order, restoring the dharma that prescribes to act in a spirit of *ahimsa* while delivering punishment. Thus the *Mahabharata* says that proper expiation can be made without killing. Similarly, Buddhism does not have a concept of god, in the same sense as in other theistic religions. Buddhism teaches that all human beings have the potential to achieve or arrive at enlightenment by their own moral and spiritual efforts and there is no need of a God to judge or to punish, or to prescribe punishment or to give authority to men to punish. Buddhist teaching, as handed down orally and then contained in various revered texts (notably the "Dhammapada"), stresses the way a human being should live in order to strive for and attain the goal of enlightenment. By contrast with other religions, the "law" of the Buddha is more like "advice" for the individual's earthly and spiritual journey, for the way to generate good *karma* (action) and, in a sense, avoid the punishment which necessarily follows wrong doing or wrongful thoughts and passions. The central idea of the Buddha's teaching is a scheme of moral and spiritual improvement, the Noble Eightfold Path, which describes what is Right View, Resolve, Speech, Action, Livelihood, Effort, Concentration and Contemplation. Right Action is set out in a number of precepts which necessarily follows wrongdoing of wrongful thoughts and passions. The first of these is to abstain from taking life. The Buddha's path is equally clear on the attitudes that will help or hinder one's progress. The injunctions on Right View and Right Resolve make it clear that there cannot be any question of acting in a spirit of revenge, of hatred or with a desire for retribution (Chatterjee and Datta, 2004, 113-158). If punishments are to be administered in accordance with Buddhist or Jainist teachings, this should be done in a spirit of compassion, aimed at helping the criminals along their path of life by correcting them, giving them a chance to do good deeds to earn merit. The right to life is recognized in the very first Precept (of the Five Precepts, namely Pancasila) that the Buddhist layman is expected to observe. It will be noted, then that Buddhist thought extends the right to life to the animal kingdom as well. In Buddhist religious life, the philosophy of *maitri and avihimsa,* universal love and nonviolence, derives its validity from this position. Since in the Buddhist context, the taking of life of even the meanest thing cannot be condoned, capital punishment is repugnant to Buddhism. Punishment should be reformatory, not punitive. All forms of retaliation are ruled out, for, as the Dhammapada says, "Hatred does not cease by hate; hatred ceases only by love; this is the eternal law". (Dh. 1.5.) The curative hypothesis of Jaina and Buddhist philosophy prescribes a unified approach that accommodates the Other to cure in a *Dharmic* (ethical) way of responsibility. The subsequent section argues how this purgative model can deterritorialize the existing law of logos to arrive at futural nomadic laws or nomos law which would be laws beyond law.

Nomos Law and Dharma: Purgativa, Contemplativa and Unitiva

Giorgio Agamben in his *State of Exception* introduced the notion of pure law which is non-sovereign in nature, or a kind of law beyond law (Agamben, 2005, 34-35). Pure law is messianic but also immanent, because it would be law that is not grounded in life, morality, scripture or institutions. In his Essay, "Force of Law", Derrida named such law beyond law "justice". He claims, "I want to insist at once to reserve the possibility of a justice, indeed of a *loi* that not only exceeds and contradicts law but also perhaps, has no relation to law."(Derrida, 2001, 231) Justice exceeds law; while every particular or determinate law is deconstructible, justice is not deconstructible. Justice is that in the name of which every law is instituted. Derrida went to the extent of saying that "deconstruction is justice." Justice is the incalculable with and for which one calculates the law (Crockett, 2012, 116). Justice represents a space beyond law, or a law beyond law by which law functions. Commenting on this messianic quality of law beyond law, Clayton Crockett in his book, *Radical Political Theology: Religion and Politics After Liberalism,* mentioned the idea of event which is the result of productive unconscious; that is, the dynamic unconscious produces events of the *a venir*. Pure law 'does not concern conscious belief, the affiliation to any belief or principle, party, position or God, but rather the unconscious Other, who mediates an event' of singularity and futurality. In *A Thousand Plateaus,* Deleuze and Guattari contrast a law based on logos with a nomadic, nomos law. Nomos is a smooth, unconscious law that contributes to deterritorialization, an absolute deterritorialization that "can be called the creator of a new earth" (Crockett, 2012, 124). Nomos Law, Crockett says is the law beyond law, or at least a form of law that exceeds bio-political control. This nomos law is unconscious in the sense of being before and beyond simple consciousness. The *Upanishad* says, *'yasmin sarvani bhutani atmaivabhud vijanatah'* i.e. that he who realizes the universal self sees all human beings as belonging to a kingdom of ends. Spirits in unity with themselves must in the end be in unity with one another. To live as selfish or cruel individuals is to jeopardize the purpose of creation. *Ahimsa* (non-violence) or fellow feeling for all living things, enfolding in its merciful arms even the lowest forms of animal life, is the natural fruit of *abhaya* or spiritual life according to the *Upanishad* (Radhakrishnan, 2010, 46). *Ahimsa paramo dharma,* i.e. non-violence is the highest *dharma,* resound in the *Mahabharata* many times and the *time-to-come* demands such a philosophy of dharma or an ethics of forgiveness which subscribe to the law beyond law, the real law of justice which cannot think of death penalty.

NOTES

Passages from the Death Penalty Seminars come from Peggy Kamuf's draft translations. 'DP1' has been used to refer to the first year of the Death Penalty Seminars, followed by the session number. Quotes and references from the Death Penalty seminars have been taken from Michael Naas' essay, "The Philosophy and Literature of the Death Penalty: Two Sides of the Same Sovereign", *The Southern Journal of Philosophy,* Vol. 50, 2012.

REFERENCES

Agamben, Giorgio, *The State of Exception*, trans. Kevin Atell, Chicago, University of Chicago Press, 2005.

Bennington, G, "Rigor; or, Stupid Uselessness", *The Southern Journal of Philosophy*, Vol. 50, 2012.

Coward, H, *Derrida and Indian Philosophy*, State University of New York Press, 1990.

Coomaraswamy, A.K, "The Vedanta and the Western Tradition" in *Perceptions of the Vedas*, ed. Vidya Nivas Misra, Indira Gandhi National Centre for the Arts, New Delhi, Manohar, 2000.

Chatterjee, S. & Datta, D. *An Introduction to Indian Philosophy*, University of Calcutta Press, Calcutta, 2004.

Crockett, C., *Radical Political Theology: Religion and Politics after Liberalism*, New York, Columbia University Press, 2011.

Derrida, Jaques, *On Forgiveness, in On Cosmopolitanism and Forgiveness*, trans. Mark Dooley and Michael Hughes, London and New York, Routledge, 2001.

Derrida, Jacques. *The Gift of Death* . 1992. Trans. David Wills. Chicago: University of Chicago Press, 1995.

Derrida, Jacques. "For What Tomorrow", A Dialogue, with Elisabeth Roudinesco. Trans. Jeff Fort. Satnford, CA, Stanford University Press, 2004.

Deutsch, Eliot, *Advaita Vedanta: A Philosophical Reconstruction*, University of Hawai Press, Honolulu, 1973.

Fritsch, Matthias, "Derrida on the Death Penalty", *The Southern Journal of Philosophy*, Vol. 50, Spindel Supplement, 2012.

Haase, U and Large, W, *Routledge Critical Thinker Series on Maurice Blanchot*, London and New York, Routledge, 2001.

Kamuf, P, "Protocol: Death Penalty Addiction", *The Southern Journal of Philosophy*, Vol. 50, Spindel Supplement, 2012.

Mascaro, J, *The Upanishads*, Delhi, Penguin, 1994.

Naas, Michael, "The Philosophy and literature of the Death Penalty: Two Sides of the Same Sovereign", *The Southern Journal of Philosophy*, Vol. 50, Spindel Supplement, 2012.

Rao, Srinivasa, *Advaita: A Contemporary Critique*, Delhi, Oxford University Press, 2012.

Radhakrishnan, S, *Eastern Religions and Western Thoughts*, Delhi, Oxford University Press, 2010.

Sadler Gregory B., "Responsibility and Moral Philosophy as a Project in Derrida's later Works", *Minerva—An Internet Journal of Philosophy* Vol. 8, 2004.

5

Deconstruction as 'Hospitality to the Other': A Derrida—Ambedkar Dialogue

The image of God is better honoured in the right given to the stranger than in symbols

(Levinas, in Derrida's *Avowing*, Weber, 2013, 29)

"Living together [vivre ensemble]*" requires doing the impossible—more than once ... [it] would thus stand as another name of the event ... [it] is an event of life; even better, "living together* [vivre ensemble] *is a matter (and manner) of living. This makes it a matter of "grace," for ... "grace grants life life for life"* [la grace accorde la vie pour la vie]

(Weber, 2013, 158)

The caste system does not demarcate racial division. The caste system is a social division of people of the same race.

(Ambedkar, 2014, 238)

Deconstruction is hospitality to the other, to the other than oneself, the other than 'its other,' to another who is beyond any 'its other.'

(Weber, 2013, 178)

"Living together [vivre ensemble]" depends on the hospitality extended in the name of "grace"—a hospitality exceeding any conditions that might me inscribed in a pact, a law, or a right. Hospitality, as an event of "grace," must remain unconditional; it must entail a willingness to exceed bounds, to cross thresholds, and to welcome an arrivant, *no matter whom or what. Such absolute hospitality requires ... that I give ... to the absolute, unknown, anonymous other, and that I give place to him, that I let him come, that I let him arrive, and take place*

> *in the place I offer him, without asking of him either reciprocity ... or even his name.* (Weber, 2013, 157)

Viewed in Derridean optic, the *iterability* of the philosophic syntagma, *Homo homini lupus* enjoins one to avow the impossible possibility of futural *arrivance / aimance—rahamim perhaps*, or of "living together [*vivre ensemble*]." This chapter seeks to situate Derrida's prolegomena on "living together" in his "Avowing—The Impossible: "Returns," Repentance, and Reconciliation, A Lesson" (2013) in the context of caste as a vicious reality of social divide. In doing that it extends Derrida's notion of *teshuvah* and *vivre ensemble* beyond their Abrahamic context so that the entire discussion of "living together" can be widened to bring in the Global South in this discursive practice. Drawing largely upon the recent work, *Living Together: Jacques Derrida's Communities of Violence and Peace* (Weber, 2013), it offers the possibility of reading Derrida's notion of "living together" or *hospitality* with B.R. Ambedkar's plea for a caste-less world or *Comitia Centuriata* (assembly of the plebeians / lower castes) as enunciated in his book *Annihilation of Caste* (Ambedkar, 1937; 2014, 228). Derrida thought of his essay on the question of "living together" primarily as a lecture to be delivered and Ambedkar too conceptualized his *Annihilation of Caste* (1937) originally as a lecture, which was however never delivered but later it came out as a classic. For centuries, the stigma of caste (a system of social structure based on the hierarchical set up of four *varnas* or *jatis* (caste) such as Brahman, Khatriya, Vaishya and Sudra or Dalit has divided Indian society and till today the political class in Indian democracy continues to capitalize on a caste-based vote bank politics which is mired in divisive discriminations on the basis of high caste or low caste origins. The caste system evolved as a division of labor (where manual and rigorous works were apportioned to the lower castes) and through centuries it rigidified into an abominable system of social compartmentalization where higher castes like the brahmins initiated the custom of untouchability to retain their own social hegemony and clout. Untouchability is the Indian version of apartheid based not on skin colour but on caste origins. The low caste people were ghettoized and brutally segregated by the brahmins who treated the former as untouchables but relied mostly on them for survival as the burden of manual labor was made to be solely carried out by the lower castes. To justify the caste system, the brahmins gave it a religious sanction citing scriptural approval (Ambedkar, 2014, 296-309). Even today, lower castes or Dalits in India remain socially alienated and estranged. Untouchability no longer exists as virulently as it used to be earlier because it has been banned through legislation but its overarching presence remains and continues to persecute the Dalits even today. Dalits are occasionally killed, stripped naked, lynched or even raped by the upper castes if they dare to go for inter caste marriages or if they violate social norms as laid down by the brahmins. B. R. Ambedkar himself belonged to the *Mahar* sub caste, one of the lowest of castes in Indian society who were primarily assigned the job of manual scavenging or cleaning of human excreta by the inhuman caste system. All through his life Ambedkar fought for social equivalence through the abolition of caste system and as India got independence in 1947, Ambedkar became the first law minister of independent India and was chiefly instrumental in drafting the Indian Constitution (drafted in 1950) that recognized caste as a crime against humanity. Ambedkar, while envisaging the Indian Constitution, was guided by the principles of justice and law and saw to it that Dalits, the lowest of the low castes in Indian society who were viewed as outcastes and untouchables for centuries get their due. Although Ambedkar was inspired by the ethos of "living together" all through his life, his provisions for the Dalits in the Indian constitution however was purely juridical and legislative in nature. His suggestions for positive discrimination and affirmative action for the low castes in the Indian Constitution have evoked a lot of controversy and continue to enrage many even today. Some even ascribe the current rise of narrow identity politics in the Indian electoral fray to his provision for positive discrimination or other identity-oriented policies of reservation for the dispossessed sections of Indian society. In other words, Ambedkar's dream of "social endosmosis" (living together, if I may say so) (Ambedkar, 2014, 260) or annihilation of caste remains a far cry as many believe that his juridical provisions for affirmative action has further accentuated the already divided Indian society—a view that deliberately overlooks the reason for such juridical measures and shy away from the vicious system of caste division that continues even today. This chapter argues that perhaps we need a combination of Derrida's philosophization of *vivre ensemble* with Ambedkar's activism for annihilation of caste to actualize the dream of an egalitarian society.

This chapter therefore attempts to read the category of caste or casteist society, Ambedkar's analysis and prescriptions for the abolition of caste system, etc through the analytical tropes of Derrida as laid down in his notions of "living together", *hospitality* and *politics of friendship*. Such conjoined reading will appear irksome to many scholars who believe that given the differences of contexts that exists between these two scholars (Derrida engaging with European reality, Ambedkar focusing on Asian or typically an Indian social order), such mutual exchanges of ideas are impossible. This chapter while acknowledging the context specifications of these two thinkers, attempt a globality of thought exchange and in doing that it emerges that Ambedkar shares a lot with what Derrida has said on social division and apart from that, both thinkers, although hailing from two completely different countries and social backdrops, betray identical thoughts vis-à-vis incidents of social estrangement. Ambedkar was expelled from upper caste Hindu society (*ensemble*) for his low caste origin, was ostracized by the predominantly high caste educational fraternity but ultimately, after incredible struggles, went to Columbia University to do his PhD at a time when higher education for a low caste boy was unthinkable in pre-independence India. Derrida too was expelled from his school for his Jewish origin and Algerian society, although not casteist by nature, had similar demographic varieties as India. Derrida himself has confessed that he could never overcome the trauma of his eviction from his Algerian school and vowed to oppose all attempts for narrow communitarianism in future. Similarly Ambedkar's lifelong commitment to annihilate the brutal practice of caste was solidified after he was atrociously thrown out of his rented home by his brahmin landlord for disguising his low caste identity. Throughout the rest of his life, Ambedkar continued his mission of analyzing the genealogy of caste, its religious and statist root and since then Ambedkar continued to deconstruct Hindu foundationalist scriptures for their sanction of caste. Ambedkar's *Annihilation of Caste* is a brilliant example of deconstruction that problematizes the metaphysics of caste in the social structure of Indian. It can be argued that a Derrida-Ambedkar dialogue is long overdue as it amounts to a perfect combination of both the theoretic and practical execution of the principle of "living together". Recent scholarship on Gramsci and postcolonialism has brought together both Gramsci and Ambedkar in the same theoretic ensemble on the question of caste as subalternity (Zene, 2013) and in a similar vein a Derrida-Ambedkar dialogue would offer an intense version of their combined radicality in forging the plank of *vivre ensemble or rahamim (compassion)*. In what follows, I would first discuss Derrida's philosophization on a futural grammar of "living together" and hospitality and subsequently I would extend that to analyse Ambedkar's plea for the abolition of caste as a category of inhuman and eternal estrangement. Derrida premised his entire *oeuvre* of "living together" primarily on the Israel-Palestine divide or on issues of European immigration, apartheid. In other words, while Derrida restricts himself (quite naturally) to the European contexts and his radical alternative suggestions of "living together" draws exclusively on Abrahamic theological or philosophical traditions, Ambedkar, on the other hand, focuses on Hindu scriptural sanctions of caste and his radical tirade against caste, although not as philosophic as Derrida, was immensely revolutionary in terms of futural vision and practical enactment of social equity. Ambedkar disowned Hinduism in a radical move and embraced Buddhism to denounce the Hindu theological endorsement of caste. Ambedkar's vehement castigation of caste and his virulent attacks against traditional Hindu religion as the origin of caste sparked off a Gandhi-Ambedkar face off as Gandhi was not in favour of critiquing Hinduism itself. While Gandhi was against caste, Gandhi's critique of casteism was allegedly status quoist (Roy, 2014). Contrary to him, Ambedkar was far more liberal and radical in his approach. The Gandhi-Ambedkar debate on caste offers a highly important document on the question of "living together" and if we situate this debate in the light of Derrida's notion of *vivre ensemble*, Gandhi appears less inventive than Ambedkar in his vision of social endosmosis.

Inventive Engagement to Avow the Impossible

For Derrida, the notion and experiences of "community" or "living together", never "ceased to harbor radical, in fact infinite interrogations." The quest to find the mechanism to live together inspired Derrida throughout his life and career to innovate concepts of *hospitality, auto-immunity* as well as on rights, law, responsibility and justice. This also led him to deconstructively unfold the tension between law and justice. Derrida's famous assertion, "deconstruction is justice" made during his address of the 1989 colloquium "Deconstruction and the Possibility of Justice" at the Cardozo Law School remains highly significant in any understanding or evaluation of juridical interventions to curb the menace of crime against humanity. Derrida's intellectual and philosophic investment in unpacking issues of law, community and justice throws up serious questions of intellectual readings in these crucial domains of civilisational future. For him,

> The intellectual's task is that of an "inventive engagement," that

> is, a "transaction that suspends the safe horizons and criteria, the existing norms and rules," in order to "analyze, to criticize, to deconstruct them ... yet without ever leaving the space empty, in other words open to the straightforward return of any power, investment, language, and so on. (Weber, 2013, 2)

The category of community and "living together" must figure at the heart of this "inventive engagement" of intellectuals and the entire philosophic orientation of both Derrida and Ambedkar testify the same. Pheng Chea and Suzanne Guerlac note in the introduction of their *Derrida and the Time of the Political*,

> Deconstruction can itself be considered an event and an activity insofar as it brings about a confrontation between philosophemes and categories of knowledge and decisive mutations in the world, causing an interruption of the former by the latter in order to force a mutation in thought so that it can be adequate to the task of thinking these important shifts, instead of being outstripped and rendered irrelevant or effete by them. (Weber, 2013, 3)

Ambedkar launches such phenomenal mutation or deconstructive interruption in traditional Indian epistemes by unpacking the fallacies of foundational Hindu scriptures. Ambedkar clearly evinces such politics of deconstruction that opens up new avenues of perceptions, avenues that seem impossible to materialize in the traditional way. Derrida's starting point in his lecture, "Avowing the Impossible: Returns, Repentance, and Reconciliation" (Weber, 2013) is the possibility that "a certain avowal would announce itself as the first commandment," and the first commandment is "living together is the acknowledgement and avowal of the impossible." (Weber, 2013, 7) Now how do we define the impossible here? William Robert, one of the contributors in the book edited by Elisabeth Weber (Weber, 2013), investigates Derrida's different notions of the "impossible". Robert elaborates on Derrida's urge for hospitality as doing the "impossible in the face of the impossible: to open, to affirm, to avow, to give, to save, to bless, to respond, to take responsibility, to welcome ... The list is necessarily endless and incalculable." (Weber, 2013, 8) The "impossible" according to Robert, generates an "eventive grammar" that effectuates a "displacement" of ontology by life (such as, for example, of "being" by "mighting") and that consequently disrupts traditional concepts of politics based on the understanding of "together" (in French, the adverb *ensemble*) as a substantive "*ensemble*" (Weber, 2013, 8-9) Derrida's contribution to this eventive grammar comprises "expressions such as "*the live-ance of life [le vivement de la vie*]," a neologism whose English translation is in fortuitous consonance with his famous *differance*, and like the latter, introduces an unheard of quality into the philosophical discourse, namely a new grammar invented according to "an originary subjunctive"—a grammar of *as if*, of potential and vitality, that names "living together [vivre ensemble]" as preceeding and exceeding any ontological "*being together [etre-ensemble]*", and thus Heidegger's "being-with" [Mitsen] (Weber, 2013, 9). In what follows we look into this non-totalitarian notion of being together that can salvage humanity from regressing into communitarian ghettos.

A-synchrony and the Totalitarian *Ensemble*

How do we envisage the contours of that eventive grammar of real "living together [vivre ensemble]" without getting trapped into the juridical or statist version of forceful living together *(etre ensemble)*? Such coercive togetherness would be far from real camaraderie, so "how to live together"? Derrida would posit an alternative, that of an anachronistic alterity,

> Living together" with the past of those who are no longer and will not be present or living, or with the unpredictable future to come [*avenir*] of those who are not yet living in the present: if this constitutes an indisputable possibility of the being-with-oneself [*etre-avec-soi*], of a living together—with one self, in a self thus shared or divided, enclosed, multiplied, or torn, open too, in any case anachronistic in its very present, at once increased and dislocated by the mourning or the promise of the other in oneself

> ... other than oneself, an Other outside of oneself in oneself, then living together no longer has the simplicity of a "living" in the present pure and simple, no more than the cohesiveness, the self-coincidence of a present whole [ensemble present] living present, present to itself, synchronous with itself, conjoined with itself, conjoined with itself in a kind of totality. (Weber, 2013, 20-21)

The alterity of past and future, the irreducible experience of memory and of the promise, of mourning and of hope, all suppose some rupture, the interruption of this identity or of this totality, this accomplishment of a presence to self—a fracturing openness in what one calls *un ensemble* [whole, gathering, ensemble], with the noun ensemble, which Derrida distinguishes here from the adverb ensemble in the expression, vivre ensemble. (Weber, 2013, 21) The adverb in the expression, "living together," appears to find its sense and dignity only there where it exceeds, dislocates, contests the authority of the noun "ensemble" ... the authority of the whole [ensemble] will always be the first threat for all "living together." And inversely, all "living together" will be the first protestation or contestation, the first testimony against the whole [*ensemble*]. (Weber, 2013, 21)

Derrida realizes the impossibility and difficulty of such a contestation and reminds us of the messianic nature of the entire venture, "living together [vivre ensemble]," well then, a certain avowal would announce itself as the first commandment."(Weber, 2013, 18) He further added,

> to avow the unavowable, let us recognize, would not be to avow. Let us avow that. The avowal, if there is one, must avow the unavowable ... an avowal, if there is such, must avow the unavowable, and forgiveness, if there is such must forgive the unforgivable—and must therefore, do the impossible. If such were the condition of living together," it would command doing the impossible. (Weber, 2013, 19)

The best of "living together", Derrida says, "is often associated with peace" but one needs to distinguish between perpetual peace or messianic peace and forced peace or armistice. (23)

Therefore, "one must live together well ... one has no choice. It is, indeed, always a matter of necessity, and therefore of law: one cannot not "live together even if one does not know how or with whom ..." (23-24). Therefore, we have to free "living together of all statutory surveillance" to allow authentic peace to come. (25) Living together does not signify mere *savoir-vivre* or an art of living, but "living together" means "living together" that suggests "understanding one another in trust, in good faith, in faith, comprehending one another, in a word, being in accord with one another." (25) But 'accord' suggests a language of the heart (Coeur), something that reminds us of the peace of "living together", a peace of justice and equity, but not under the law of law, in the sense of legality, of law [droit], or political contract. Derrida believes, "the love or peace of the heart, the fiancé [of confiance, confidence, trust promise] accord or concord, exceeds the contract guaranteed by law or state legislation." (26) It becomes more clear when he says:

> This "living together" even where it is irreducible to the statutory or institutional ... bond, opens another dimension to the same necessity—and that is why I have spoken of the other, of the stranger, of the hospitality to the wholly other who exceeds the statutory convention. The "good" of the "living well together" supposes the interruption of the natural as well as conventional relation; it supposes even this interruption tout court that one calls absolute solitude, separation ... (26)

"Living together" supposes therefore, an interrupting excess both with regard to statutory convention, to law and with regard to symbiosis, to a symbiotic gregarious, or fusional living together. (26-27) It is reducible neither to organic symbiosis nor to the juridico political contract. Derrida would suppose a rupture with identitarian and totalizing belonging that rests on the idea of a homogeneous whole [*ensemble*]. (28) Derridean "living together" "supposes and guards, as its very condition, the possibility of this singular, secret, inviolable separation from which alone a stranger accords himself to a stranger, in hospitality

> Where the "living together [*ensemble*]" (the adverb) contest the completion, the closure, and the cohesiveness of an ensemble (the noun, the substantive), of a substantial closed ensemble identical to itself; to recognize that there is "living together" only there where ... it welcomes dissymmetry, anachrony, non-reciprocity with an other who is greater ... (28)

This brings us to the question of hospitality because it thrives on this unconditional non-reciprocity.

Teshuvah and Hospitality

If hospitality is the "deconstruction of the at-home; deconstruction is hospitality to the other, to the other than oneself, the other than "its other," to an other who is beyond any "its other."

Any ideal of the "living together" must begin with this deconstruction of the "at-home." Ipseity of the ethnos must give way to the other, the brahmin must open up to the dalit because that summarises the ethics of *dharma*, the grace or eventive grammar of living together. Derrida refers to Levinas who recalled that, "The respect for the stranger and the sanctification of the name of the Eternal are strangely equivalent. And all the rest is dead letter ... the image of the God is better honoured in the right given to the stranger than in symbols. "(29) As any "juridico-political founding of a living together is by essence, violent" (29) one must strive and avow for the possibility of the impossible and avow the unavowable and therefore, the "living together" that Derrida is proposing goes beyond any ensemble and therefore there cannot be a prescriptive rule bound mechanism of the 'how' of "how to live together." There is, "in any case no "how" that could take the form of precepts, of rules, of norms, or previous criteria ... the "how" must be invented by each at each moment."(34) Must we forgive the age old atrocities meted out in the name of caste, class, race or religion and move ahead or should there be a condition of repentance (*teshuvah*) on the part of the perpetrator? But all conditional "living together is no living and the notion of *teshuvah* apart from signifying repentance can also be translated as "return, or relation with God." If repentance brings proximity to god, hospitality to the other, unconditional compassion (*rahamim*) to the estranged ensures *vivre ensemble*. Derrida's late writings on hospitality offers an extended meditation on how one should relate to the stranger (French, *etranger*). The stranger is viewed as non-autochthonus, non-indigenous. If the question of how one relates to the stranger is central to any ethics of living well together, then Derrida's propositions, commandments become highly important. One commentator while discussing Derrida's avowal in the context of the Indian social discord between the Hindus and Muslims referred to Zygmunt Bauman's work on the stranger. Bauman differentiates between two types of unfamiliar, the first is the foreigner who lives in remote lands and hence spatially and territorially separated from us. The second type is the stranger who refuses to stay away from a faraway land and "hence defies the easy expedient of spatial or temporal segregation. The stranger comes into the life-world and settles here ... (84) None of these non-autochthonous and interstitial figures of the stranger and the foreigner however can explain the category of caste. A low caste person is neither spatially far away, nor has he come to stay forcefully, he is the native inhabitant, but excluded from the high caste ensemble on the basis of caste, made a stranger. Both Derrida and Ambedkar dwell on this construction of the stranger that takes place through a practice of social defamiliarization and institutional exclusion. It constitutes the notion of the outside, the dalit as the outside of the high caste *varna* fold. Priya Kumar in her comments on Derrida's notion of "living together" had to say the following

> The other is welcome to the extent that he respects the *chez-soi*—the "being-at-home of my home"- that he adjusts to the order of the house, the language, the nation state. Hospitality thus rests upon claims of property ownership and a reaffirmation of the host's mastery. This "despotic sovereignty" of the host is

> intrinsically related to ipseity, the same of the self-same. Hence the question of hospitality is also the question of ipseity; relying on how we relate to others. "The law of identity or the "being-oneself in one's own home" thus becomes the very condition of gift and hospitality." Derrida therefore "locates a violent contradiction inherent in the very condition of hospitality: The host must be assured of his sovereignty over the space he opens up to the other ... it is this aporetic paralysis at the very threshold of hospitality that must be overcome; hence hospitality can only take place beyond our pre-comprehension of hospitality. (Weber, 2013, 100)

Can the Brahmin overcome this aporetic paralysis at the threshold of hospitality for the Dalit? Ambedkar was not at all sure about that and he therefore leaned more towards the droit, legislative sanctions in favour of the Dalits so that all trajectories of ipseity can be quelled. The Derridean notion of hospitality is a great philosophization of the ethics of opening up, something that would have bolstered Ambedkar in his life long fight against caste. Like Derrida, Ambedkar too would have loved to think that

> I open up my home and that I gave not only to the foreigner ... but also to absolute, unknown, anonymous other, and that I give place to them, that I let them come, that I let them arrive, and take place in the place I offer them, without asking of them either reciprocity (either entering into a pact) or even their names. (Weber, 2013, 100)

This is a clear indication of the fact that the "experience of hospitality is co-extensive with ethics itself: "in so far as it has to do with the ethos, that is the residence, one's home ... inasmuch as it is a manner of being there, the manner in which we relate to ourselves and others, to others as our own or as foreigners, ethics is hospitality." (101)We have to therefore radically rethink, our notion of identity, home and autocthony

> Why would the friend be like a brother? Let us dream of a friendship which goes beyond this proximity of the congeneric double, beyond parenthood, the most as well as the least natural

> of parenthoods, when it leaves its signature, from the outset, on the name as on a double mirror of such a couple. Let us ask ourselves what would then be the politics of such a 'beyond the principle of fraternity'. (Derrida, 2005, viii)

The concept of politics almost always announces itself with some sort of "adherence of the State to the family, without what we will call a *schematic* of filiation: stock, genus or species, sex *(Geschlecht)*, blood, birth, nature, nation—autochthonal or not, tellurian or not." If hospitality is ethics, then a new politics of non-filiation is required. Ambedkar's version of Dalit politics can be viewed as an attempt towards that.

Conclusion: Associated Living/*Rahamim Perhaps*

In the beginning was the end and we began by "living together as "grace" as an "event" in life. Derrida's grace is Ambedkar's social prestige and emancipation of the Dalits. Constitutional safeguards alone cannot ensure "living together" for the Dalits and Ambedkar realized that fully well, one therefore looks for excess of the juridical mechanism, looks for *rahamim*, compassion, the unconditional hospitality that does not mind whether the opponent or the stranger is repentant or not. Such unconditional reaching out as theorized by Derrida is echoed in what Ambedkar said in his dream of an ideal Indian society,

> An ideal society should be mobile, should be full of channels for conveying a change taking place in one part to other parts. In an ideal society there should be many interests consciously communicated and shared. There should be varied and free points of contact with other modes of association. In other words there should be social endosmosis. That is fraternity which is another name for democracy. Democracy is not merely a form of government. It is primarily a mode of associated living, of conjoint communicated experience. It is essentially an attitude of respect and reverence towards fellow men." (Ambedkar, 2014, 260)

Such conjoint communicated experience and associated living that generate *rahamim* or respect for fellow beings is the real "living together." In that way, Derrida and Ambedkar are co-travelers in the same quest of *vivre ensemble*.

NOTES

(Ambedkar's *Annihilation of Caste* was originally published in 1937 but all references here have been taken from the 2014 critical edition of the same).

REFERENCES

Ambedkar, B.R. *Annihilation of Caste*, The Annotated Critical Edition with an Introduction by Arundhati Roy, Navayana, New Delhi, 2014.

Derrida, J, *The Politics of Friendship*, Verso, New York and London, 2005.

Weber, Elisabeth, ed. *Living Together: Jacques Derrida's Communities of Violence*, New York, Fordham University press, 2013.

Zene, Cosimo, ed. *The Political Philosophies of Antonio Gramsci and B. R. Ambedkar*, London and New York, Routledge, 2013.

6

Being With and Inter-Beings of Flat-Ontology: Poetry After the Anthropocene

'The animal looks at us, and we are naked before it. Thinking perhaps begins there.' (Atterton and Calarco 2004, 122).

'If not from these animals, where will wisdom arise?'
(Serres 2001, 124, 125)

Poetizing beastly tales or philosophizing on the *non-human* has been theorized earlier and in most of these cases the animal figured in the poematic to cater either to childish narratives of fun or sometimes as metaphoric agents, however, poetry or philosophy has seldom regarded the question of the animal as little more than a sub-topic or a *Caliban-topic,* if I may use such a term to signify the subservience of animals. Philosophy has only coronated the human and philosophically, human beings own the world and are accorded the sovereign universal locus. Throughout much of the history of metaphysics -- from Aristotle to Aquinas, from Descartes to Kant, and from Hegel to Husserl—the essence of the human has been repeatedly determined in opposition to the animal, where the former is understood to be in possession of a certain capacity or trait such as logos, ratio, Will, spirit, Being, subjectivity, etc.—qualities which the *non-human* lacks. Contemporary paradigms of posthumanism critically question these essentialist determinations of the human, a project that seeks to continue and deepen the efforts of the so-called "hermeneutists of suspicion" of the 19th and 20th century.

Jeremy Bentham, in a short passage from his *Principles of Morals and Legislation*, first published in the revolutionary year 1789 (and also reprinted in *The Animals Reader*), announced devastatingly that philosophers who worry (as they continue to do on every front) about the capacities of animals, about whether animals can speak, reason, plan, remember, exhibit kindness, and so on, are asking a wrong or irrelevant question. The question to be asked, according to him, is 'can they suffer?' While one shudders at such animal apathy or such common instances of consolidation of anthropocentrism, one also encounters a heartwarming counter-narrative of animal respect from Jacques Derrida who in his *L'Animal que donc je suis* or *The Animal That Therefore I Am* (2009) rallies for a 'zoo-auto-bio-bibliography' (*L'animal autobiographique*) or a *renaissance of Beasts that restores our deepening respect for the non-human*. Neologisms such as 'zooësis' (Chaudhuri, 2007); 'zoontology' (Scholtmeijer, 1997; Wolfe, 2003), 'zoopoetics' (Atterton and Calarco, 2004, 115); 'humanimality' (Surya, 2001) unfurl a whole new horizon of epistemic renascence. Deleuze and Guattari's theorization on *'becoming-animal'* in *A Thousand Plateaus,* (lycanthropes) and Jean-Luc Nancy's non-anthropocentric notion of *being-with* are other such instances of radical reopening of the non-human *dasein*. Initially I shall engage with recent works in this field that make a detour through new optics of critical animal studies, something that makes our discussion of humanimality and poetry easier because these recent works are now assigning respect and attributes to non-humans which we traditionally denied them. In what follows, I shall initially engage here with two recent works in this field namely, *Creaturely Love: How Desire Makes us More and Less than Human*, Dominic Pettman, 2017; *Creaturely Cosmologies: Why Metaphysics Matters for Animal and Planetary Liberation*, Brianne Donaldson, 2015. Any discussion on poetry and philosophy in the Anthropocene must have a detour through the different ontological questions and critical thoughts raised in these two important works. Having discussed the radical openings enunciated in these two works, I shall prepare the argumentative optic for greater ontological egalitarianism in which the non-human will be elevated to the same philosophical height—something I will show poetry can demonstrate.

Ontological Multiplicity: "Being with and Being-Together"

Recent theorisations of Dominic Pettman and Brianne Donaldson as mentioned above, are significant contributions in the domain of Critical Animal Studies and Planetary Studies as both launch a substantial critique of speciesism or species exceptionalism. While the first book deflates and deconstructs the anthropological claim about love being an exclusively human attribute, the second book deanthropologizes the mission further by decentering the human through an exposition of creaturely cosmologies in which the category of the human is located within other creaturely multiplicities. Both the authors adopt counter-philosophic responses to challenge philosophy's anthropocentric bias that has led to the problems of the Anthropocene. While Pettman would rely on Ovid, Nietzsche, Deleuze, Salome, and others, Brianne Donaldson banked on Jainism and Whitehead's Process philosophy to constitute her non-anthropocentric creaturely cosmology. Pettman begins by narrating how for both Freud and Berlant, love is a "sublimated form of libidinal attachment" and in similar vein the Christian distinction between Eros and Agape continues even today in secular and popular forms. For Bataille, however, love is simply a more intense version of erotic experience. Pettman thus traces the different ways in which the concept of love has established itself in Western discursive practices revolving around Eros and civilization as Love is still venerated as spiritual, while desire is sneered as merely physical. In the beginning the author tries different definitions of love and problematizes the normative distinction between love and desire, where love is elevated as sublime human quality, while desire is carnal and animal like. This leads to the primary research question: "Do animals experience love?... do they have the symbolic wherewithal to upgrade mere attraction into the aesthetic exception of love?" (Pettman, 7) In a similar vein, another question is raised: do those animals that call themselves human experience love? If the answer is yes, then what does this key term and the expression of this experience—in different narratives, image formations, etc— tell us about our "animal inheritance"? We, humans generally use the term 'creature' to inferiorise animals, or to belittle a 'figure of abjection' that is a mere animal or a monster and from such conventional attitude springs the "dominant and official narrative of Western culture that has always been an elaborate disavowal of our creaturely life" through the assertion of what Agamben called the "anthropological machine". Pettman defies this anthropocentric bias and argues that "on a certain level all eyelashes are eyelashes, whether they are connected to a pig, a dog, a giraffe, a human or an elephant ... a profound kinship within or despite vast and undeniable biological and ontological differences" (Pettman, 8). This is an attempt therefore to focus on the possible "shared nature of being", or on "being with and being-together". To perceive therefore the creaturely aspect of ourselves is not to simply reduce the human to the animal or the opposite to elevate the animal up to the human but to introspect on what Bernard Steigler calls the "the non-inhuman within the inhuman-being" (Pettman, 8). Viewed from the religious angle of St. Augustine, the term 'creaturely love' signifies a spiritual lack. Seen through the Christian scholastic lens, love is something which is not redeeming as it is "temporal and material, thus mortal, human all too human." So the notion of creaturely love can never be disembedded from its religious connotations and it also proves how our acts of love were sacralized and authorized through the disciplining of the libido. Pettman concludes that "there are traces of divine libidinal economy in all earthly loves" (Pettman, 12). From here Pettman approaches both modern and premodern thinkers on the question of creaturely love and schematically he visits first the moderns such as Nietzsche, Salome, Rilke, Balthus, Proust, etc and subsequently goes back to Fourier, Fournival, medieval folktales and the poet Ovid and also to contemporary films to trace the themes of creaturely love. Modernists, Pettman shows, have raised some important queries on this count, problematizing in that way the very idea of the human. How is our humanity different from our animal heritage or legacy? How does human sexuality characterize our "species being"? This book, by raising these questions, aims to "foreground the importance of the animal figure in the canonical Western discourse of love and desire" (Pettman, 14). Pettman refers to the film *The Turin Horse* (2011) that captures Nietzsche's well known traumatized state after he witnessed a horse being tortured. Nietzsche's seminal works such as *Genealogy of Morals* and *Human, All Too Human* have strong totemic aspects that enlist "figural and symbolic animals from his countermoral system—eagles, lions, asses, and so on" (Pettman, 16). Even Freud too viewed the horse as a totemic creature, which on many occasions figured in neurotic or psychotic narratives revolving around what Freud called the "anxiety animals" (Pettman, 17). Freud even used the horse as his own symbol for the *id* itself as it is a powerful and yet unruly animal that necessitates the disciplining mechanism of the superego. For Freud then, all humans are "centaurs" and horses have inherently libidinal or erotic connotations and they emerge as one of the primary totems of libidinal economies in general. So animals are "good to think with" as Levi Strauss famously maintained and mythical creatures help us to challenge traditional ways of looking into the human-animal divide. Pettman refers here to Vanessa Lemm's book on Nietzsche's "animal Philosophy" that identified the centaur as a "meta-hybrid, a centaur with wings and thus divided three ways by animal, human and angel" (Pettman, 18). Pettman observes that the "centaur is thus a figure that helps us explore the sly existence, dormant power, and erotic techne of what I would like to call "creaturely love," that is, the nonhuman, ahuman, more-or-less-than-human passion or affect that attracts us to the other in a register beyond or outside the conventional discourse of soul mates" (Pettman, 18).

Creaturely Continuum

All these points signify the "creaturely continuum" we inhabit on a very material and actual register with other life forms and the cultural or symbolic meanings that we, humans, democratically ascribe to animals really helps subverting the human exceptionalism. The rest of the book deepens this horizontality of creaturely continuum that does not allow the supremacy of the human species over other non-human "creatures". Pettman's discussion on "Groping for an Opening: Rilke between Animal and Angel", therefore, discusses Rilke's notion of the "Open" by which he implied "the free, actual, immediate, immanent stream of Being" unhindered and unfiltered by human self-consciousness. Rilke's "open occurs outside the walls of the prison house of language—outside the interpreted world." (Pettman, 22) Only the "epiphanic shock of love" can help us to glimpse the Open, the state of "atemporal bliss", something that the animal, according to Rilke, has the privileged access, as Pettman quotes Rilke saying,

> *...we know what is really out there only from*
> *the animals' gaze; for we take the very young*
> *child and force it around, so that it sees*
> *objects—not the Open, which is so*
> *deep in animals' faces...* (Pettman, 22)

If that be the case, then Rilke asks in his Ninth Elegy, why do we "still insist on being human" as our human bias takes us further away from the "pure unthinking ecstasy of the lark and the tiger, the gnat and the bat?" In this connection, Pettman reminds us that Nietzsche "wanted to be a flogged horse" in the company of Salome the lover and Rilke emphasized "his own animality, his own creaturely love" for Salome. The Centaur then is an ideal though paradoxical figure that symbolizes humanity living in harmony with its animal side. The book is actually suggesting here an "ontological moat between animal and human" (Pettman, 25) and although we always emphasize the human element in matters of the heart, there are artistic acknowledgement of the creaturely source of intense passion or creaturely instinct that leads us to the "immanence of the Open". The conclusion we arrive at is that the "metaphysical surplus of the linguistic animal" (i.e. the human) is to be opposed to attain that creaturely freedom of the Rilkian Open—"That is what fate means: to be opposite/ to be opposite and nothing else, forever" (Pettman, 25).

From Nietzsche and Rilke, the author now approaches Robert Musil, who has been called "a prose Rilke" and who also talked of love's "disavowed creaturely aspect" and two of his short stories, which Pettman refers to, suggest that "human sexuality is but a heartbeat away from a bestial passion", although unbridled lust has always traditionally been associated with animality in all Western discourses that distinguishes between Man and Beast. Musil problematizes the reductive dichotomy of animal-body versus human-soul by a project of "transindividuation" that foregrounds the animal aspect of human sexuality and makes us see ourselves as "first and foremost kinfolk of the beasts" (41). For Musil, animals "are people too: an ongoing realization that needs to be re-realized every day, lest it be erased and effaced by the conscientious workings of the anthropological machine" (42). To reiterate his point, Pettman now goes to the distant past, referring to Richard de Fournival's "Bestiary of Love", which was composed in France in the middle of the 13th century that combined two genres of bestiary lore and epistolary romance. Fournival's slim book is shown here as making an important contribution to the human understanding of creaturely love and Fournival's menagerie underscores the "shared characteristics between lover and animal" (55). Fournival is portrayed as revolutionary for his time as he proves that love "activities of a man and a woman are by implication assimilable (and often inferior!) to the characteristics of so-called lower animals... moreover love is not necessarily presented as a noble calling but as a crow picking out a man's brain through his eye sockets" (Pettman, 55-56). Through this "zoological approach to Eros" and through an "iteration of Aesop's fables", Fournival, according to Pettman, makes clear the creaturely core of human desire (58).

Flat-ontology, Ovid's *Metamorphosis and* Elliptical Poetics

The fixity of modern human species being is always opposed to the fluidity of the medieval species-being that resonates with the cosmology whereby a creature can metamorphose into something or somewhat radically different or combines into wonderful hybrids in popular imagination. Such "propoto-zoological" imaginaries are available in Ovid's Metamorphoses, where a woman can suddenly get morphed into a tree, a bear, a bird, etc. The author finds in Ovid a classic case of the human/non-human indistinction as in Ovid we see how our Gods are fascinated to enjoy disguising into specific animals such as rams, bulls, swans, horses, etc to manipulate ordinary mortals. Ovid's world therefore is "radically in flux" and enunciates a "radically unstable ontology" that abandons our notions of "settled being" (Pettman, 73). Ovid provides brilliant examples of creaturely love in his poetic renditions and in him too we get examples of the hermaphrodite which is described as male or female, that is, who seems to be neither and both. This suggests a new human fusion or an exceptional transgendered figure. This leads Pettman to conclude that Nature, since ancient times, evinces a "queer heterotopia", "pink in tooth and claw" (Pettman, 78). Ovid's universe then is animated by constant change or by "a fickle metaphysics" (Pettman, 81). Ovid, Pettman rightly claims, renders his stories in such a way that metaphors are literally transfigured. So when someone is described as acting like a "wounded bull" is virtually turned into a wounded bull. Hence the

> analogical miraculously becomes the actual ... reality and its

> representation collapse together and fuse ... and ... it captures a truth at the heart of creaturely love. Human passions are not simply like animalistic ones but are indeed an expression of them. Alterity is not only an excluded other but a latent aspect of identity ... (82)

Viewed from this Ovidian optic, "we are all anagrams of each other" and Ovid's unique world argues for "an unfinished universality ... in which every phenomenal form rhymes with many others and everything derives from the same flesh" (Pettman, 82). All these are pointing towards some ontological bridging that leads to transductive possibilities. Pettman brilliantly engages with different philosophical takes on life and living that can explain all these varied claims of ontological difference and repetition. In doing this, the author rightly refers to Manuel DeLanda's notion of "flat ontology" that does not negate material differences but emphasizes the "non-hierarchical nature of What Is". What Ovid does, therefore, is to remind us that "all recognizable figures in this world, of this earth, can be placed within the one, same demographic category" (Pettman, 84). Seen from this angle, "Moths become flying leaves" and "butterflies are flying flowers" and in this context the book refers to Agamben's notion of the "elliptical poetics" that shows how language becomes mimetic of its subject

> the mysteries of being, and being-with. It is also proleptic in the sense that it anticipates "the hieroglyph of a new in-humanity" that it seeks to bring into being, through incantation. Such words thus perform the idiom of the coming community which cannot be pinned down or identified. (Pettman, 88)

One marvels at the idea of such a coming community of new "in-humanity" where the human-creature hierarchy is demolished and being emboldened to imagine such imagined community of human-creature enmeshing we may adopt the Deleuzian lens to see that a "distinction between human, satyr, seal, or seductive software is a provisional and contextual one, soon to be dissolved by a different assemblage in the passage of time. Humans are thus exposed as merely one type of any number of cosmic "desiring machines" (Pettman, 105). The canon of human normativity is thus subverted and the conclusion of the book sums it up on how we can queer the canon and citing Plato's Symposium, the author reminds us how "love is to be found in all animals and plants, and ... in all that is; is not merely an affection of the soul of man towards the fair, or towards anything. Eros ... was considered a vital force uniting all creatures—indeed, creation itself (Pettman, 108). So the old Freudian distinction between (animal) instinct and (human) drive takes a beating in view of the discussion we had so far because this book is speaking of a "shared affective heritage between all creatures, manifested to be sure in very different ways" (Pettman, 109). So the primary objective of Pettman is not to argue "that humans and animals are one, in some great Cosmic love-in; ... [but to argue] that all loves are creaturely" (Pettman, 110). The foreclosure of our species-being leads to species hierarchies but we forget that "Humans are human in so far as they are an animal caught up in a process of hominization: the ongoing evolutionary, historical, and technical trajectory of the species. This process is ongoing, improvised, immanent and without clear direction or destiny" (Pettman, 110). So the end remains open, yes the Rilkean Open.

> Pettman's theorisation testifies how the notion of creaturely love consolidates the paradigm of the anthropologiocal machine but for Pettman creaturely love is his term for the "anthropocentric ambivalence that lies at the heart of the dominant discourse on desire." The "image repertoire" of love relies on animal metaphors and allegories and the idea of creaturely love is oxymoronic as nonhumans, we claim, do not love the way we do symbolically or linguistically but at the same time the idea of creaturely love challenges such chauvinistic species exceptionalism because the sovereign supremacy of the homo zoon logon is also challenged by ontological overlaps between humans and animals (Pettman, 111).

This leads to the idea of ontological inter-enmeshing, and in Brianne Donaldson this idea of ontological continuum and creaturely inter-connectedness is further actualised through her recourse to Jainsim, Process theory of Whitehead and poststructural thoughts of Derrida and Giles Deleuze.

Ontological Conviviality and Coming Community of Inter-Beings

If Pettman prepares us for this coming community of ontological overlaps, Brianne Donaldson in her book, *Creaturely Cosmologies: Why Metaphysics Matters for Animal and Planetary Liberation* (2015) seeks to foreground a similar agenda of ontological conviviality by foregrounding the pervasive subjugation of animals in western thought. Such animal subjugation has been sanctioned, she claims, just because they are animals and Brianne critiques such circular logic of justified human domination throughout her works. Initially we are given statistical accounts of how ten billion birds and land mammals were slaughtered in 2012 alone in the United States to cater to human needs and how such slaughterings are justified as killings and abuse of animal are naturalized everywhere. Donaldson rightly observes,

> majority of global societies endorse the capture, transport, torture, breeding, selling and killing of creatures in unthinkable numbers and by grotesque means primarily because their captive bodies or disembodied flesh, fur, and fluids are highly desired, highly profitable and because their suffering is discounted and out of sight. (Donaldson, x)

So humanity colonizes/kills animals because they are animals. In fact the legitimization of animal killing is so deeply entrenched that any contrary logic fails to gather larger support. However, as we dethrone the category of the human in our analysis of the Anthropocene, a deeper engagement with philosophies of non-harm to other non-human beings as well as to the planet Earth assumes great significance. Donaldson's argument exactly does that by offering two metaphysical insights that challenge the anthropo-centric logic of animal subjugation by offering alternative planetary vision, namely the Indian philosophical tradition of Jainism and the Process relational worldview as enunciated by Alfred North Whitehead. Predominant Western World views in science, religion, philosophy, and politics universally "privilege human experience, knowledge and senses ... as the authoritative lens through which to judge our vast universe" (Donaldson, xii) and to negate such man-centric hegemonies, Donaldson distinguishes between "biased metaphysics" that advocates human supremacy and alternative "adequate metaphysics" that adopts a broader planetary approach to all creatures. Rather than moving towards post-metaphysical times, we should, Donaldson suggests, look for better metaphysical approaches that make us see how animals and other non-human creatures whom we exclude are historically and ontologically entangled with us and with whom we can collectively co-create the future of the planet. Donaldson would call the ancient Indian philosophical vision of Jainism that advocates non-harm to all entities and the Process relational thought of Whitehead as "creaturely cosmologies" because "they begin their analysis not by unequivocally privileging a specific understanding of human senses or desires but by seeking to explain those senses and desires through the broader active creaturely multiplicity" (Donaldosn, xiv). Jainism begins with the notion of the "Jiva" that signifies a core vital force that sustains all life-forms. Both these metaphysical standpoints envisage "the creaturely multitudes" that animate the buzzing universe. Viewed from the perspective of Jainism and Process philosophy, every creature appears to be in a continuous process of unification between what is and what might be. Life happens, as Donaldson says, in these Deleuzian "ontological gaps" between "things, interbeing, intermezzo" (Donaldosn, xvii). Our present state of being therefore is a "joint or hinge" between our past and the intangible future. For Donaldson, Jainism and Whitehead's Process-relational thought posits every creature as such a hinge. Creaturely cosmologies provide a metaphysical grounding to socially, ethically, and politically affirm the value of individuals and communities currently excluded by humanistic hegemonic frames. Donaldson's primary argument seems to be that any notion of planetary future would require radical transformative ways of living and thinking with our fellow citizens. Hence veganism alone would not suffice to constitute the alternative vision for creaturely multiplicity. Here Brianne would refer to Steve Best's idea of radical reformation of animal liberation philosophy that sees the project of human animal, non-human animal, and earth liberation as inseparable projects. So our personal decisions to abstain from eating animal flesh and animal products, while highly laudable, are not adequate enough to transform our overall and fundamental attitude towards nonhuman fellow creatures and hence our veganism is to be supplemented "with cross-disciplinary and cross-movement engagement with broader systemic issues affecting creaturely life and our collective planetary future" (Donaldson, xix).

Proto-ontology, Inverse-Ontology and the Closures of Species-Being

In a climate of anti-developmentalism in which we reject all Western normative, transcendent, humanist, and andocentric metaphysical bias, it is not sufficient to advocate such rejection of scientism or profit-oriented reason. To gather greater progress now, we also require, according to Donaldson, "fundamental inversions, dispersions, and reversals ... into the realms of ontology, epistemology, action and discourse" (Donaldson, xix). Her whole theoretic argument is a quest for such inverse-ontology and counter-discourse. Like Pettman, the all-important question Brianne raises is: should we continue to get trapped within the closures of our fixed species being which is characterized by humanist, subjectivist, gendered, nationalist categories or we embrace cosmologies that deconstruct these categorical essentialism for a wildly abundant multiplicity of life in its creative becoming. Donaldson revisits the newly emerging domain of critical animal studies by addressing three existing standpoints on animal studies such as the theories of identity, Difference, and Indistinction-based approaches to the human-animal question. Referring to Derrida and Judith Butler, both of whom have contributed in critical animal studies by rejecting the metaphysical approach, Donaldson would argue that one needs to "drive straight into this metaphysical gap to recover and develop alternate ontological accounts sufficient for our creaturely and planetary multiplicity" (Donaldson, xxi). She would engage with Whitehead's Process-relational philosophy to underline the subversive features of "panexperientialism" as enunciated by Whitehead. Here she elaborates on the idea of "intra-action", a term she borrows from feminist physicist, Karen Barad, and which comes out as the "central ontological/ epistemological/ethical theme that shapes [her] entire project" (Donaldson, xxi). Different aspects of Jain philosophy is discussed to bring to our notice the "intra-active" implications of Jainsim and Process philosophy respectively. The Jianist notion of Ahimsa (non-violence), and Deleuze & Guattari and Donna Haraway's post-humanist frames are used to actualize a "re-worlding" towards alternate futures.

Brianne's analysis on critical animal studies rallies for a "radical social approach to veganism and animal rights that transcends bourgeoisie liberalism" that leads to "post-hierarchical world views and democratic and ecological societies" (Donaldson, 4). The traditional onto-political ways of looking into the human animal question that emphasizes on identity-based optics are critiqued to advocate a "proto-ontological" vision where the "proto-ontological" extends to Derrida's insight

> to the way we categorize the entire living world. Before we can even talk about what it means for you or I, a black man, a woman, a child with disability or an animal to "be", we must recognize that we are already in networks of relationships, intra-actions,

> perception, ... and response that happen before we can divide the world into categories of race, gender, function or species. The proto-ontological plane includes those aspects of the ontos, or being that exist outside our current knowledge regimes, categories or thought. (Donaldson, 11)

Brianne's entire theoretic schema consolidates this notion of intra-action and the Indistinction based approach to animal theory signifies "the messy plane of proto-ontological relations that destabilizes the human/animal divide ..." (Donaldson, 11). Western metaphysics since Plato has relied on an essentialist approach of identity and hence fails to grasp this proto-ontological notion of inter-relation. Donaldson looks for alternative metaphysical traditions that allow such intra-action to happen. In her attempt to find new cosmologies of living, Donaldson would bring in Derrida's gestures towards a wider metaphysical scope beyond the "phenomenological subject-as-presence". Derrida envisages our ontological condition of life as more primordial than subjectivity, by replacing the 'who' by a 'how'. For Donaldson, this shift from the 'who' to the 'how' is an intrinsic aspect of creaturely cosmology because "[h]ow is a processive verb that is underway in the ongoing development of the living in general." Derrida, according to Donaldson, here moves from a logic of difference to processes of *differance* that are at work everywhere that means beyond humanity. In a brilliant articulation of Derridian philosophy of difference, Donaldson perfectly captures the central point when she says

> Life is a verb of becoming or ... nouns with perpetually destabilizing movement, an experience of opening. Derrida demonstrate that a how does not fit well into any political, personal, juridical, ethical or democratic framework, each of which demands a responsible who ... Derrida turns away from active subjects to interrogate "different modes of the conception-appropriation-assimilation" of the other. (Donaldson, 18)

In this context, Donaldson also engages with Judith Butler who she argues, in spite of her "personal commitment toward precarious life, is never able to theorize a cosmology wide enough to conceive of the truly strange. Though she troubles the human-animal binary through her difference-based approach, she fails to move towards a theory of indistinction" (Donaldson, 21). Drawing on ideas of "cross-species conviviality" and "neighborliness" towards "fellow inhabitants of the world", Donaldson looks into metaphysical systems that can positively affirm the complicated, the lively, chaosmic multiplicity that results when the binary is levelled (27). This would lead to the paradigm of "co-feeling and com-passion". Subsequently Brianne unfolds as a wonderful exposition and application of Process philosophy to accentuate her thesis for creaturely cosmologies. Conjoining the ideas of Deleuze, Guattari and Whitehead, she underscores Deleuze's theory of 'becoming animal', where he appreciated Whitehead for his process thoughts. Deleuze's rhizomatic speculations explored the becoming of events as the "anarchic replacement for the stasis of being" (Donaldson, 30). She perfectly applies this Deleuzian nomadism of non-stasis for her project of creaturely pluralism because we can in this way "co-create our world" in the process of becoming that would result in a "democracy of fellow creatures" (Donaldson, 43). Brianne's focus on Jain philosophical stance of Ahimsa or non-harm to all creatures is perfectly relevant here and through a reference to Jain ideas of *Jiva, Anekantavada or Nayavada and Syavada,* she elucidates Jainism's emphasis on multiple perspectives that can help in the formation of panexperientialism. Having elaborately discussed the two metaphysical streams of Process philosophy and Jainism, she synthesizes the two standpoints by showing how Jainism and Process describe "the creative advance of creaturely life as one of active becoming rather than static being" (Donaldson, 75).

In an attempt to decipher the deeper connotations of these philosophical ideas to substantiate her position, Donaldson narrates how the Jainist idea of the *Jiva* is "immanent and constitutive of its very indistinct and fluid identity. The actual occasion and *Jiva* do not do an action as pre-formed actors. Rather, they are the intra-active relation between what is given and what is possible" (Donaldosn, 76). Based on her studies of Jainism, she perfectly uses Jainist *Ahimsa* in her exposition of post-hierarchal society of planetary future when

> *Ahimsa* is not a doctrine that applies only to some fixed categories of life. Rather it is the practice of freedom that unifies every becoming with the broader universe of perceptive and provocative creatures, however strange and different they may be. *Ahimsa* is a direct intra-action aimed at proliferating all liberties ... the science of peace is a two sided bridge between what is and what might be in every becoming. Ahimsa is always the dialectical intra-action of an indeterminate entity aiming toward fuller perception and deeper experience of the multiplicity. (Donaldson, 90)

This is indeed brilliant stuff and a perfect fusion of Jainist *Ahimsa* with objective of planetary becoming. If Jainism provides one version of the intra-action, then Process thoughts emerge as another form of intra-active becoming for Donaldson. Borrowing Whitehead, Haraway, and Deleuze, she explains how the notion of species is "far from the fixity of the biological discipline ... species like the body are internally oxymoronic, full of their own others ... [a kind of Whiteheadian creative multi-species crowd." (Donaldson, 101). We may recall here Pettman's reference to Ovid's discussion of ontological fluidity and this is how the project of creaturely love and creaturely cosmologies merge together. This is according to Donaldson also akin to Deleuzian "zone of exchange ... in which something of one passes into the other" (Donaldson, 102). Such zones of exchanges are possible if we adopt Deleuze's call for the "nonphilosophical" or the "prephilosophical" and doing philosophy with the nonphilosophical is to actualize the idea of the "becoming minoritarian" or "becoming animal", "becoming woman"—a disruptive act through which we can subvert hegemonic discourses and fixed identities. Donaldson quotes Deleuze and Guattari: "The philosopher must become nonphilosopher so that nonphilosophy becomes the earth and the people of philosophy" (Donaldson, 103). So, "becoming-with" means tolerating differences so that we can co-shape the future with non-human creatures. Through these prolonged philosophical discussions, Brianne tries to show that

> animal and planetary liberation must include the freedom of concepts as much as the freedom of bodies and the creaturely cosmologies of both Process and Jainism offer a provocative vision beyond loss, towards a future when that which has been excluded can be revalued in the present within transformative becoming of greater stature, prehension and co-feeling. (Donaldson,113)

Brianne, in her own words, has "tried to think with and through these lesser known metaphysical systems so that they might become something else in our philosophical future ... for the sake of its transformation and the overhaul of our collective life ways" (Donaldson, 132). Her argument has without doubt created a "de/re/territorialisation of critical animal studies that can affirm a panexperiential universe. In what follows I shall demonstrate how poetry can actualise such deterritorilisation of thinking through a reference to Indian English poetry.

Panexperientialism and Poetry

So far I have tried to build the argument that anthropocentric ways of conceptualizing our Being is the root cause of all ontological closures that leads to violence and creaturely separation and in my detailed analysis of the theoretical standpoints of Pettman and Donaldson I have tried to forge the reverse-ontological view of panexperientialism, a paradigm that holds a key to our future in all post-anthropocentric theorization and in this section I will show that poetry has the power to translate that into reality. I shall focus on a recent book of poems which is named after the fox, the non-human, the agent of the *human-other* and interestingly enough the book opens with a reference to Ted Hughes` celebrated poem, *Thought Fox*. This book *Fox Land and Other Poems* by Bishnupada Ray (2016) comes within the genre of Indian English poetry and in what follows I shall undertake a close analysis of some of the poems contained in this book to understand how it deconstructs the idea of human supremacy. For Ted Hughes, as for other non-anthropocentric philosophers whom I have mentioned already, fox, the non-human signifier configures the transcendental or the immanent, the plexus of gnosis, the cobwebs of the nomadic. Such sublimation and expansion of the signifier may entail one to say—'The fox is the poem, the poem is the fox.' (Webster, 1984)

There is one critical opinion that Hughes's fox has none of the freedom of an animal. It cannot get up from the page and walk off to nuzzle its young cubs or do foxy things behind the poet's back. It cannot even die in its own mortal, animal way. The reason is it is the poet's creature, wholly owned and possessed by him, fashioned almost egotistically in order to proclaim not its own reality but that of its imaginatively omnipotent creator. The critical opinion confesses that this view was originally written before coming across Hughes's own discussion of the poem in his *Poetry in the Making* - 'So, you see, in some ways my fox is better than an ordinary fox. It will live forever, it will never suffer from hunger or hounds. I have it with me wherever I go. And I made it. And all through imagining it clearly enough and finding the living words' (Hughes, 1967).

The fox is no longer a formless stirring somewhere in the dark depths of the bodily imagination; it has been coaxed out of the darkness and into full consciousness -'The window is starless still; the clock ticks,/The page is printed.'—The fox is the poem, and the poem is the fox. (Webster, 1984) This is how the fox, the non-human borders onto the poetic, the noematic content of the *non-human* is sublimated to the non-defined to the ineffable, non-closure. The fox-land coalesces into the land of *dichtung*. In his *Che cos'è la poesie (henceforth CCP)* Derrida problematises a series of linguistic binaries, the first of which concerns poetry and prose. Derrida's primary task was to define poetry, but he indicates that this is 'impossible because definition is a philosophical exercise rather than a poetic one. If one tries to force poetry to render an account of itself, it enters a prosaic mode and destroys its essence as poetry. Poetry therefore cannot communicate what it is to anyone'. The metaphor Derrida uses to explain this is that of a hedgehog trying to cross a road. The hedgehog starts out toward the other side (say, the "prosaic side"), but half-way there it sees danger and curls up to protect itself. The curling up is an inward action of turning back on itself, metaphorizing the inability of poetry to define itself without referring back to itself. The irony of the curling up is that, if the danger is an oncoming car (say, Derrida's deconstruction-mobile), the hedgehog will be destroyed precisely because it does curl up. By referring only to itself, poetry is unable to access the "other side of the road" and therefore cannot be an adequate means of communication.

This danger of deconstruction is therefore the primary dilemma of Derrida's essay "Che cos'è la poesie?". Language attempts to achieve reality and cannot do so; yet, insofar as it fails to do so, it deconstructs itself and is destroyed. Derrida by comparing a poem to a hedgehog, means to suggest that interpretation means attempting the impossible, a perilous traversing of the road, an ever 'denied translation' (Derrida, CCP 291), with the hedgehog always escaping, always in retreat or defensively rolled up, and hardly visible before you hit and destroy it. 'Translate me, watch, keep me yet awhile, get going, save yourself, let's get off the autoroute' (CCP 295), pleads Derrida's hedgehog, suggesting that we should nevertheless make an effort to watch for it, and try to take it off the road and into our heart. Despite the protective needles which serve to discourage us from breaking through its defenses, despite its vulnerability, and its disappearance in the very question—'What is poetry?, the hedgehog bears and sustains the promise of mystery and teaches us the heart' (Derrida CCP 299). One may call a poem that very thing that teaches the heart, invents the heart, *that which*, finally, the word *heart* seems to mean and which Derrida argues, exploring the multiple semantic resonances of the phrase, *learn it by heart*, which names both interiority and exteriority of poetic knowing: 'the independent spontaneity, the freedom to affect oneself actively by reproducing the beloved trace' (CCP 295). For Derrida, this nature of poetry enables it to exist beyond rigid oppositions, closed cultural contexts, critical frames and the thick web of logocentric categorizations. Questioning the separateness of such categories as reason and rhetoric, argument and heightened aesthetic sensibility, the hedgehog 'disable[s] memory, disarm[s] culture, know[s] how to forget knowledge and set fire to the library of poetics' (Derrida CCP 299). Through the highway metaphor Derrida signals several things. The first one is the epistemological orientation of poetry, the hedgehog's remaining always close to the ground, and the essence of the human experience. The hedgehog is directed both outward and inward, simultaneously suggesting the fragility of its position as well as its estrangement from and ill adaptedness to the depoeticized contemporary world. Derrida's metaphorical highway undoubtedly also embraces the established and habitual ways of thinking and writing about poetry which 'throw the hedgehog onto the road' (CCP 289), only to flatten, frame and run it over in a desire to fix its meaning in an absolute unique form (CCP 293), to tame its otherness and unveil all its guarded secrets. Through its relation to the heart and its consequent power to affect the reader and to shape his cognitive and emotive rapport with the world and language, the hedgehog also denotes the poem as an act of communication and translation. The reader of a poem, in Derrida's view, can be both a guardian and an intruder of its secrets; a comfortable resident in its often uncomfortable space, at ease with its gaps, stumbling blocks and murky grounds, and a relentless searcher after and an uncoverer of truth, desiring its complete unconcealedness, struggling with the poem's difficult, broken or failed communications.

Given that, Bishnupada Roy's new book, *Fox Land and Other*

Poems (2016) is a unique attempt to enshrine the hedgehog, the fox, i.e. the poetic in this de-poeticised world. Bishnu in his earlier books of poems has already touched upon issues related to the everyday, the ephemeral and the epiphenomenal as well as the primordial, but this new attempt on his part to encode the *labenswelt of living* in a semantic and symbolic menagerie of the *fox land* transpires into the Derridean hedgehogic nuances of the heart.

For Bishnu, in his book *Fox Land and Other poems* (2016) under this new poematic schema, "the jottings of my pain/ defamiliarises the nights/that we make to turn this place/ as sublime as foxly possible.' When the fox measures up to the sublime, one awakens to the animal soul, their agonies dawn to our deafened, indifferent cogito and we hear the non-human say, "you are smart we know but/do not play the minority card/the politics of appeasement/please give us back our corridor/our forest our food our freedom/take away your trains/and population/you like to ride the elephant/but you ride the tiger/by taking us for a ride". Bishnu traces the genesis of the poetic self to the moment of human hubris gone on a colonizing/killing spree—"a cozy little dove is on the roof/of our sentimental home/shoot at him and make him fall/and a poet is born with a lyric cry/out of the anthills of life"

But the lyric cry generates a greater sense of the void, "for the dove has a face/of a dear child, an angst/with which we live and die/in spite of our broken world/this emptiness in the eye/is just an emptiness/of having the sky/and also not having it/the animal song now/is no compensation/so we have chosen/our apocalypse of mist/and drizzle and dead moon/and a rare cold hill village/called Jatinga"—(Jatinga happens to be the village known for the unusual incidents of bird(poet) self-killing). The hiatus of having the sky and yet not having it underscores Bishnu's testament of the cactus land where "we cannot grow on favourable ground/living through ages of hostility and evil/we are comfortable with this parched soil/any friendly rain brings about/a quick blossoming effect/which is not good for the world/this articulation of evil through cactus shape/is our only chance to regain innocence/who then enjoy the flowers of my toil/ yes that's what happens to an ass/like me and I shall bray myself hoarse/to the full of my throat and heart/when I am full sick of my dick". Such protestations of the underdog, such assertion of the *sub-human, non-human* gets further accentuated when Bishnu would remind us, "product is a closed category/ like the bourgeois or the rich/and daunting like a pantheon/ with heavy glass doors and windows/of distinction class and shibboleth/the process of making or building/or moving from rags to riches/or to settle down at the ladder/is far more comfortable to see/or to write or to grow up with/so that the entire life goes/to make up a painstaking ontology/*that which exists through itself/is what is called the meaning*/like wearing of animal fur/and letting the animal go naked/into the/ night of transcendental feeling." Is it an attempt to redefine the subaltern here? To recategorise the have-nots? For "every bullock there is a yoke/nay a bullock is made for a yoke/nay a bullock is married to a yoke/nay a bullock is castrated for marriage/nay marriage castrates a bullock".

But in the smithy of the ordeal called life, in the precipice of the gloom, the poet salvages the effusion, rescues the light, "this darkness beneath the lamp/makes me desperate for light/the light that can consume all the darkness I gather/all the ugliness I gather/at my ontological hermeneutics/like the picture of Dorian Gray/in a slingshot of apocalypse/I find myself at the outskirts/from where I look at my life/just a dot of light I can see/and nothing else to talk about." In Fox land, this is foxly possible, to talk of the light, even though "just a dot of light" amidst the encircling gloom, and from the dark emerges the fox, from the abyss, the hedgehog of poetry, from the zoontology, the zooesis of life. Prospero the Human warms up to the swearing non-human, Caliban converges with the fox, poetry begins.

REFERENCES

Atterton, Peter, and Calarco, Matthew, eds., *Animal Philosophy: Essential Readings in Continental Thought*. London and New York: Continuum, 2004.

Chaudhuri, Una (2007). '(De)Facing the Animals: Zooësis and Performance.' *TDR: The Drama Review*, 51, 8-20, 2007.

Derrida, Jacques, *L'Animal que donc je suis*. ed., Marie-Louise Mallet. Paris: Galilée.

---------------- (2002). 'This Animal That Therefore I Am (More to Follow).' Trans. David Wills. *Critical Inquiry*, 28, 369-418, 2006.

Donaldson, Brianne, *Creaturely Cosmologies: Why Metaphysics Matters for Animal and Planetary Liberation*, Lexington Books, 2015.

Fudge, Erica, ed., *Renaissance Beasts: Of Animals, Humans and Other Wonderful Creatures*. Urbana and Chicago: University of Illinois Press, 2004.

Kalof, Linda, and Fitzgerald, Amy, eds., *The Animals Reader: The Essential Classic and Contemporary Writings*. Oxford and New York: Berg, 2007.

Nussbaum, Martha (2006). *Frontiers of Justice: Disability, Nationality, Species Membership*. Cambridge, Mass.: Belknap Press, 2006.

Pettman, Dominic, *Creaturely Love: How Desire Makes Us More and Less Than Human*, University of Minnesota Press, 2017.

Ray, Bishnupada, *Fox land and Other Poems*, Brown Critic, Delhi, 2016.

Serres, Michel, *Hominescence: Essais*. Paris: Le Pommier, 2001.

Scholtmeijer, Marian, 'What is "Human"? Metaphysics and Zoontology in Flaubert and Surya, Michel, *Humanimalité: l'inéliminable animalité de l'homme*. Paris: Néant, 2001.

Webster, Richard, " 'The Thought Fox' and the Poetry of Ted Hughes", *Critical Quarterly*, 1984, accessed through http://www.richardwebster.net/tedhughes.html

Wolfe, Cary, ed., *Zoontologies: The Question of the Animal*. Minneapolis: University of Minnesota Press, 2003.

7

Geology of Morals or Auto-Deconstruction: What Comes After the Anthropocene?

This chapter takes the two seminal essays of Dipesh Chakrabarty published in *Critical Inquiry*, "Climate and Capital: On Conjoined Histories" (2014) and "The Climate of History: Four Theses" (2009) as its point of departure to argue for a new post-anthropocentric imaginary in the domain of critical theory. In doing this it draws largely on available templates of radical French thinking as enunciated by Giles Deleuze, Jacques Derrida, Helen Cixous and Jean Luc Nancy and also on recent theoretic trajectories of new disciplines such as Critical Animal Studies (Calarco, 2008; 2015), Posthumanism (Wolfe, 2010; Braidotti, 2013) and New Materialism (Crockett and Robbins, 2012), etc. All these new thought currents go beyond the Anthropocentric paradigm to unpack new road maps for future through innovative ideas of ethics, subjectivity, energy, theology and politics and any deliberation of post-Anthropocentrism must incorporate these radical optics to constitute a grammar of counter-epistemology of the future. In asserting my propositions further, I would begin by referring to Dipesh Chakrabarty's concern for a new model of 'deep history' only to mount a critique of his apocalyptic observations on geo-centrism and planet studies. I would argue that while Chakrabarty is absolutely right in drawing our collective attention to the anthropomorphic bias of all existing historiographic or political economic epistemes and also perfectly justified in his reiterated demand for inaugurating a new genre of planet history or species history to understand the implications of the Anthropocene, he fails to walk the extra mile to incorporate a genuine deconstructive approach to the problem. He goes near and yet shies away from the crux of the matter, and in that way misses the real implications of the whole task. His whole endeavor in both his essays seems to be only to project the inefficacy of our normative analytical modes of political economy. There is no denying that we need to recognize now the enormity of the planetary and geological changes, and yet we are powerless to ward off cosmic upheavals. All that we can do is to replace our existing political economic and sociological structures and habits which are accentuating geological changes. Chakrabarty seems to deny that. The Anthropocene necessitates a restructuring of our conventional imaginaries so far as our ideologies, consumption patterns and ontological orientations to others are concerned. In Chakrabarty we merely get the articulation of a genuine concern for the fallout of the Anthropocene but his over-prioritization of planet history over geo-political or political economic praxis can be seriously questioned on the ground of repetitiousness, closure and lack of futural directions. His notion of species history or his proposition for an earth saving politics to avert the anthropogenic climate change is pertinent but not adequate enough to constitute a real paradigm shift in humanities and social sciences. For attaining that, I would argue, we need to go to radical French thinking on post-subjective critical theory and also to the proponents of critical animal studies or zoomorphic zoontologies who have been raising these points on a requisite earth centric 'geology of morals' or humanimality to dislodge the hegemony of the humanist logic that sees the earth and other species as subservient to human needs. At the end of his paper, Chakrabarty speaks of 'Enlightenment reason' as the savior that can salvage us from the apocalyptic doomsday arising out of global warming but radical French thinking has exactly ascribed all anthropogenic aberrations to the instrumentality of Enlightenment reason and its associative logic of human sovereignty that resulted in the hubris of the human cogito and the annihilation of the other species and geological resources.

This chapter therefore approaches the crisis of the Anthropocene through posthumanist and New Materialist optics as provided by Giles Deleuze, Jacques Derrida, Crockett & Robbins and Helen Cixous. Drawing primarily on recent works in these fields such as *The Reject: Community, Politics and Religion after the Subject* (Goh, 2015) and *The Animal Question in Deconstruction* (Turner, 2014); *Religion Politics and the Earth: The New Materialism* (Crockett and Robbins, 2012), etc this paper posits for a futural thinking of the Derridean *khora,* the 'non-ground' that thinks beyond (auto-reject) our anthropocentric or anthropomorphic aspects, a project that incorporates non-human animals, their voices and silences. If the *khora* allows the "impossible possibility" of the arrival of the *other,* then we can think of the animal-other, the absolute alterity, or as Derrida called it, the "divinanimality" that "breaks with [...] the similar, to situate oneself at least in a place of alterity radical enough whereby one must break with all identification with an image of oneself, ... with all humanity." (Goh, 2015, 233) In this context, Helen Cixous` notion of the "counter Bible" or the animal perspective or the "animots" look highly relevant. Such animotisation would be our "second innocence" animating divine *jouissance.* Can we then think of a future discourse of politics/survival strategy in the Anthropocene centering on the non-human or the animal? I would also argue for the Deleuzean idea of "becoming non-human", or the "becoming animal" for radical survival possibilities in the Anthropocene. This impossible figure can be the animal, as the animal has always been rejected as a possible figure of thought in politics or political philosophy. "Becoming-animal" is that trajectory of resistance and to adopt the idea of *becoming animal* we need to "push existing political thought beyond its anthropologic and/or anthropocentric limits." The particular feeling or sensation of animal affects may perhaps be found in the originary and communicative *aisthesis* that humans and animals share. To cross the adjacent space of the animal is a question of recovering the originary *aesthesis* that is recovering the sensation of the earth milieu, of *aisthesis* that humans and animals originarily share. Originary *aisthesis* was lost when "Aristotle supplemented it with the anthropocentric logos in his political philosophy." (Goh, 230) *Aisthesis* in its immediate sensing and communication of pain or wrong done to a human or animal/ecology is of political potentiality, that is *aisthesis* in itself is already adequate to demand an addressing of the wrong committed against a human or animal or the Earth. Aristotle however refused to recognize the political potential of *aisthesis*. To recover *aesthesis*, before it is supplemented by a form of logos that has been appropriated by and reduced to the human is not only a way toward the adjacent space of *becoming animal*, but is also an unveiling of *becoming animal's* potentiality for a future political project of justice. This brings us to posthumanism, to ideas of anthropomorphic others or "earth others", to "zoo-morphic" paradigms. "Critical anthropomorphism" looks into contemporary French thought's idea of the "*clinamen*" which is clearly evident in the works of Michael Seres, Deleuze and Guattari and Nancy. "Clinamen" is some sort of subtractive thinking that debunks the capitalist accumulative impulse that drives the thought of the human subject, or subjectivity. In other words, the thought of the *clinamen* takes into account the fact that "one is always already in the process of auto-rejecting some part of oneself, even though this takes place at a molecular or atomic scale." (Goh, 2015, 233) For a posthumanism that continues the poststructuralist deconstruction of the capitalist subject, *clinamen* can be its point of departure to a world of auto-subtraction/rejection for multiple dissonances to exist. Dipesh Chakrabarty's apocalyptic apprehensions, though completely justified could have been supplemented with such configurations of futural thoughts and his repeated harping on the inadequacy of capitalist history and the requisite primacy of species history would be taken up for a critical analysis in the subsequent section to demonstrate the inadequacy of his own futural openings.

Species History, Human History and the Retention of the Anthropogenic Paradigm

Slavoj Zizek in his *Living in the End Times* (2010) has critically engaged with Chakrabarty's thesis in his "The Climate of History : Four Theses" (2009) on the ground that Chakrabarty while prioritising the global warming crisis has actually downplayed the role of global capital in initiating this ensuing disaster and Zizek also found fault with the latter's understanding of Hegelian dialectic while enunciating the anthropocentric crisis. In his paper published in 2009, Chakrabarty came up with four theses—one, on anthropogenic climate change that subverts the age old distinction between Natural history and Human history, second, on the idea of the Anthropocene, the new geological epoch in which humans emerge as the new geological force, third on the proposed dialogue between global histories of capital with the Species history of Humans, and lastly on the inadequacy of traditional humanist historical paradigms. Chakrabarty rightly begins by foregrounding the impending gloom as played out by climatologists who envisage a "World without Us" to save the planet from destruction as recent trends of global warming has a lot to do with human greed and thoughtless developmentalism. Such a crisis of course necessitates a reformulation of our epistemic registers as traditional historical or theoretic optics are ill-equipped to deal with the required analytics to understand global climate change. Chakrabarty observes

> climate change challenges not only the ideas about the human that usually sustain the discipline of history but also the analytic strategies that postcolonial and postimperial historians have deployed in the last two decades in response to ... decolonization and globalization. (Chakrabarty, 2009, 198)

He went on observing that existing Marxist analysis of capital, subaltern studies and postcolonial criticism of the last twenty-five years have been largely useful in studying globalization and yet their analytical mode failed to prepare him "for making sense of this planetary conjuncture within which humanity finds itself today." (Chakrabarty, 2009, 199) His first thesis recounts as its title suggests the gradual solidification of the humanist discourse of history since the time of Giambattista Vico, Hobbes and Croce. Following their legacy, the human centric notion of history became entrenched in our common understanding and people came to accept the fact that "all history properly so called is the history of human affairs." (203) In recent times however, if we are to believe the proponents of anthropocentrism, the "human being has become something larger than the simple biological agent that he or she always has been. Humans now wield a geological force." (Chakrabarty, 206) It is really surprising to see that while Chakrabarty raises the valid point of the erroneous humanist hegemony of historiography he shies away from transcending it completely. His call for 'species history' does not sound radical enough when placed against contemporary radical French thinkers who has dethroned the humanist paradigm completely in their theorization of the 'reject' or auto-deconstruction to unveil a post-subjective idea of history. I would comment on this in detail in the subsequent sections. So Chakrabarty, while critiquing anthropomorphic history, remains largely within it and the limits of his hypothesis come to our notice when at the end of his second thesis on the Anthropocene he refers to the "Enlightenment (that is, reason)" as he says, "Logically then, in the era of the Anthropocene, we need the Enlightenment (that is, reason) even more than in the past." (Chakrabarty, 211) However moments later he qualifies his earlier statement by saying that

> Scientists` hope that reason will guide us out of the present predicament is reminiscent of the social opposition between myth of Science and actual politics of the sciences that Bruno Latour discusses in his Politics of Nature ... the very science

> of global warming produces of necessity political imperatives. (Chakrabarty, 211)

Chakrabarty however decides not to sustain this logic or to elaborate on this new political imperative, something which New Materialists or French Post-humanists or Critical animal studies thinkers have done. The next thesis on the conversation between Species history and the Global history of capital launches an attack on the idea of putting capitalism on the driver's seat in explaining all our predicaments

> Capitalist globalization exists, so should its critiques. But these critiques do not give us an adequate hold on human history once we accept that the crisis of climate change is here with us and may exist as part of this planet for much longer than capitalism or long after capitalism has undergone many more historic mutations. The problematic of globalization allows us to read climate change only as a crisis of capitalist management. While there is no denying that climate change has profoundly to do with the history of capital, a critique that is only a critique of capital is not sufficient for addressing questions relating to human history once the crisis of climate change has been acknowledged and the Anthropocene has begun to loom on the horizon of our present. The geologic now of the Anthropocene has become entangled with the now of human history. (Chakrabarty, 212)

We need to look at us as species and it is true that this word 'species' has never occurred in standard history or political economic analysis of globalization as history has always been the recorded history of humans, and Species history on the other hand belongs to the domain of deep history and hence

> The task of placing, historically, the crisis of climate change thus requires us to bring together intellectual formations that are somewhat in tension with each other: the planetary and the global; deep and recorded histories; species thinking and critiques of capital. (Chakrabarty, 213)

This tension of divergent disciplinary pulls is a healthy sign and the inter-cognitive dialogue / multilogue is definitely a way forward but again Chakrabrty relies on reason to attain this.

Citing climatologists, he refers to their call for 'Kantian reason' to forge the plank of new knowledge and "the knowledge in question is the knowledge of humans as a species, a species dependent on other species for its own existence, a part of the general history of life." (Chakrabarty, 219)

The penultimate thesis of Chakrabarty concludes by reiterating our lack of sense of the species. He rightly says,

> Who is the we? We humans never experience ourselves as a species. We can only intellectually comprehend or infer the existence of the human species but never experience it as such. There could be no phenomenology of us as a species. (Chakrabarty, 220)

Immediately after this however Chakrabarty once again debunks the analytical tools provided by conventional history and political economy for their inadequacy, without caring to see if his own optic itself suffers from inadequacy as he harps on the same tune but cares not to give a direction for future. As we go to radical French thinking in search of alternative directions we realize that such species thinking has been doing the rounds for long. Chakrabarty's recent essay "Climate and Capital: On Conjoined Histories" (2014) repeats what he said in his previous essay and this time the emphasis is more on the question of capitalism and his refutation of Zizek's accusation against him. Surprisingly again although he makes us conscious of our disastrous impact on the planet system, he moves again within the apocalyptic closure and decides not to offer a way out. Referring to David Archer's book, *The Long Thaw: How Humans are Changing the Next 1000,000 Years of Earth's Climate* (2009), he critiques the prioritization of humans over other species as the fact remains that the planet does not put us humans first in its scheme of things and yet while making such legitimate observations once again he merely repeats what he has been saying again and again on the insufficiency of prevalent political economic parallax views

> the analytics of capital (or of the market), while necessary, are insufficient instruments in helping us come to grips with

> anthropogenic climate change. I will go on to conclude by proposing that the climate crisis makes visible an emergent but critical distinction between the global and the planetary that will need to be explored further in order to develop a perspective on the human meaning(s) of global warming. (Chakrabarty, 2014, 4)

In spite of referring again to Sunita Narain's endorsement of the notion of 'climate capitalism', Chakrabarty questions the full efficacy of such ideas which were originally propounded by Peter Newell and Matthew Paterson who insisted that

> despite often being talked about as a scientific question, climate change is first and foremost a deeply political and moral issue." And the "ecological rift is at bottom the product of a social rift, the domination of human being by human being. The driving force is a society based on class, inequality, and acquisition without end. (Chakrabarty, 2014, 9)

Narain and Agarwal's booklet titled *Global Warming in an Unequal World: A Case of Environmental Colonialism* (1991) is also referred to by Chakrabarty to register the "valid questions about historical inequalities" in global conditions but this recognition is immediately accompanied by his refrain, "but reducing the problem of climate change to that of capitalism (folded into the histories of modern European expansion and empires) only blinds us to the nature of our present, a present defined by the coming together of the relatively short-term process of human history and other much long-term processes that belong to earth systems history and the history of life on the planet." (Chakrabarty, 2014, 11) The rest of the paper voices his concern for other species as they are being hounded by humans and in due course he once again deconstructs the prioritization of humans over other species without forgetting of course to play out the pet refrain of "The climate crisis reveals the sudden coming together—the enjambment, if you will—of the usually separated syntactic orders or recorded and deep histories of the human kind, of species history and the history of the earth systems ..." (Chakrabarty, 2014, 15) This enjambment leads him to realize again that the warmed earth requires a new ethics, an ethics of humbling the hubris of the human and here Lovelock's stern message in his *The Vanishing Face of Gaia* (2009) is also cited by him, "to consider the health of the Earth without the constraint that the welfare of humankind comes first ..." (Lovelock, 2009, 35-36) In spite of raising such pertinent issues, Chakrabarty decides to end the essay not with a neat road map of the new ethics, but with a rebuttal of Zizek on the question of capitalism

> But Zizek puts capitalism in the driver's seat; it is the part that now determines the whole. My proposition is different: ... not to say that human history is the driver of these large scale processes. These latter processes continue over scales of space and time that are much larger than those of capitalism... the problems of anthropogenic climate change could not have been predicted from within the usual frameworks deployed to study the logics of capital. (Chakrabarty, 2014, 21)

So we need, Chakrabarty says "an earth bound imagination" which is undisputedly true but he prefers not to clarify on what that might be. The climate crisis he says "is about waking up to the rude shock of the planet's otherness." (Chakrabarty, 2014, 23) but he is surprisingly indifferent to the necessity of awakening to our immediate others, the animals. Chakrabarty's theses are germane to our understanding of the severity of the Anthropocene and the consequent responsibilities of future studies but they fail to provide any direction. For that we have to engage with radical poststructuralist French thought and other forms of experimental theoretic optics which do not downplay the role of capitalism and yet offer fresh insights for future while recognizing the severity of the Anthropocene. In what follows then I would engage with the posthumanist notion of the 'reject' or the 'auto-reject' to provide a road map away from conventional imaginaries of humanist templates. In doing that I would largely draw on recent books such as *The Reject: Community, Politics, and Religion after the Subject* (2015) and *Thinking through Animals: Identity, Difference, Indistinction* (2015).

N-1 Community or Becoming Animal/Divinanimality or *Khora*: What Comes After the Subject?

The post-anthropocene phase of life demands new trajectories of thinking so far as the idea of self, community, ontology, politics and ethics are concerned. Radical French poststructuralist thinkers had thought about the absolutism of the humanistic frame long back and their quest for post-subjective or post-humanist ontologies are more than relevant now and in what follows I would dwell on radical French philosophical ideas of post-humanism as enunciated in a recent book by Irving Goh. In a certain way, the present day geo-political conditions make us all *rejects*, either we reject others socially and politically, ontologically or we get rejected by others and that makes the category of the *reject* so important for us and Irving Goh's book, *The Reject: Community, Politics and Religion after the Subject* (2015) as the title suggests, philosophizes on the theoretic category of the *reject* through the radical philosophic optics of contemporary French thoughts. Goh takes Jean Luc Nancy's poststructural inquiry made in the 1960s about "what comes after the subject"—a question that Nancy posed to his leading contemporaries such as Derrida, Deleuze or Alain Badiou and many others who grappled with the poststructural problematic of the liquidation of the 'soverign subject' and its radical consequences—as his point of departure. Goh critically engages with some of the rejoinders to Nancy's question and while evaluating those answers offers its own idea of the *reject* or the 'auto-reject' which Goh argues, perfectly subtends all the radical responses to Nancy's question as provided by Derrida, Deleuze, Badiou, even by Nancy himself, or by Helen Cixous and others who theorized the possibilities of post-subjective configurations.

Borrowing from Goh, I would argue, that as post-structuralism is very much a story of the *reject*, it is worthwhile to enunciate this paradigm of the *reject* with French thoughts and in doing this I would elucidate the "philosophical, ethical and political potentialities of the *reject* and their implications for the contemporary world." (xii) Seen in this spirit, therefore, the *reject* is to be placed as a "critical figure of thought" in the post-Anthropocentric world of capitalo-democratic politics that promotes the ethos of subjective sovereignty and consequent totalisation of human power. Through his engagement with the varied responses to Nancy's question, Goh has probed to establish how many of them fall short of real post-subjective imaginaries and subsequently asserts his own notion of the *reject* which he claims has the contours of genuine post-subjective trajectories. Goh would contend that almost all radical French thinkers such as Derrida, Deleuze, Helen Cixous and others in their theorization actually bordered onto the *reject* or the notion of the "auto-reject" to envisage our thoughts beyond the sovereign subject. In Goh's analysis however, it is Deleuze and Guattari and Nancy himself who should be credited the most for upholding the idea of the *reject* in their conceptualization of radical post-humanist paradigms. The term *reject* is "but a shorthand for a theory that seeks to articulate and affirm a figure of thought that would give expression to the multiplicity of heterogeneous rejects"—they are figures who break away from all normative configurations. Goh cites the "nomadic war machine" (Deleuze), the "clinamen" (Nancy), the idea of the "becoming animal" (Deleuze), "Zoo-morphic" (Braidotti), the "animot"(Cixous), the "divinanimalite" (Derrida), "animal messaiah" (Cixous) etc—as prefiguration of the *reject*.

Deleuze's response to Nancy rallied for the construction of "new functions and discover new fields that make [the subject] useless or inadequate" and Derrida's opinion was, one could free oneself from "the necessity to keep at all cost the word subject ..." (Goh, 2) As Irving Goh goes back to Nancy's question and attempts an adequate answer, it claims that such an answer, remains the unfinished task of contemporary French thought and the radical figure of thought in French theory that "comes after the subject" can establish French theory's relevance to the contemporary world. Here Goh refers to Cary Wolfe's views in the book *What is Posthumanism?* which reiterates that the future of posthumanism or posthuman discourse can "take a leaf from contemporary French thought's question—who comes after the subject?" (Goh, 4)

There appears to be a marked rise or resurrection of the subject with the assertion of all anthropomorphic paradigms and other forms of sovereignty across the globe and therefore devising a new figure of thought other than the classical notion of the subject can emerge as a viable strategy. Critical trajectories in the domain of feminism and postcolonial studies have been instrumental in critiquing the absolutist subject and in its discussion on the coming form of religion in the postsecular world, on friendship, communities and love, Goh promotes the idea of the "auto-reject" as that new form of future. By proposing the theory of the *reject* or the *auto-reject* as a possible replacement of the totalizing subject, Irving Goh offers a theory of new ethics. Auto-rejection according to him

> involves creative regeneration, therefore, ... not self-annihilation. (Goh, 7)
>
> Giving up all that one has prepared and gathered for oneself, and giving up the position on which one has begun to ground or found oneself with all that one has gathered: that is what the subject is unable or reluctant to do. The auto-reject meanwhile detaches or frees itself from such gathering and (self-)positioning. (Goh, 8)

The ethical force of the auto-reject derives from its erasure of its sovereignty and in that way it affirms the respect for the other.

> the auto-reject, unlike the subject, has no interest in accumulating for itself predicates that might contribute to its foundation; it has no interest in totalizing everything, including elements outside of itself, within its grasp and control ... has no interest either in whatsoever foundation of itself ... (Goh, 8)

While elucidating on the notion of the *reject*, Goh argues that the idea of *reject* is not exclusively his conjuration, in fact the *reject* "has always subtended philosophy" (Goh,13), it was already with philosophy right at its beginning and is evident in both Plato and Socrates and it traverses philosophy even after them. Descartes rejected the erstwhile episteme and Hegel rejected Kant and Fichte and then in the twentieth century Deleuze rejected Hegel, a little later, Badiou rejected Deleuze, Derrida and other poststructuralist thinkers. So the story of the *reject* goes on. I however do not claim here to analyse the *reject* in the entire history of philosophy, rather I would choose my focus to philosophise the *reject* that subtends contemporary French thought. Exemplifying the *reject*, contemporary French thought envisage new forms of friendship, community, love or the politics-to-come. It also visualizes the postsecular that entails a peaceful co-existence of the religious and the secular and the posthuman future that sees beyond the anthropocentric, denying in that way any acculturation, taming, or reining in of others and their radical differences. The different ideas of radicality as posited by Goh such as "(after) friendship", "love", and "community" trace the presence of *reject* in French thoughts in reformulating our idea of community and human bond. Nancy's and Bataille's call for a "community without subject" initiates the discussion here and Heidegger's postulation of *Dasein* or *Mitsein* are rearticulated through Nancy's philosophy of community as "co-presence" or "comparution of beings" or being-in-common. In that scheme the subject is viewed as opening itself "instantaneously onto a community. In this connection, Agamben's notion of the *coming community* is also mentioned as Agamben takes the challenge of Nancy's idea of a community without presupposition and without the subject and proposes the singularity of the "whatever being." (Goh, 29) This force of the 'whatever' frees a being from all adherences to class or other determining boundaries of definiteness and such a freedom reminds us of the *auto-reject*. The "ipseity of the subject or subjectivity, with its predicates that define its distinction from others, is evacuated here... [and] whatever beings through the fact that they exist alongside one another, "form a community without affirming an identity" (Goh, 30)

This also comes closer to Derrida's logic in his *Politics of Friendship* and to Deleuze's concept of nomadology. Both these thinkers reject the normative definition of community or friendship and provide the philosophical force to mobilize the *reject* to combat the contemporary network centric "doxa of friendship, love and community". The "techno-social structure" of "communicative sociability" of today is vehemently critiqued by both Derrida and Deleuze so that such hegemonic structures can be deconstructed and that deconstructive urge is "auto-rejection". This rejection of traditional and popular forms of friendship can only be sustained by eliciting the figure of the *reject* in Derrida, Deleuze and other contemporary French thinkers. Derrida's breakage or rupture of friendship in his notion of *nouvelle aimance,* "reinstates love as constitutive l'aimance" or new forms of love that renames friendship which can even endorse the doxa of solitariness within friendship.

In tune with this, in Deleuzean philosophy too, we come across his figure of the *reject*—the lone philosopher whom Deleuze calls the '*homo tantum*'. (Goh, 61) Both Deleuze and Guattari would postulate here the emergence of a new future relation between beings—"The creation of concepts in itself calls for a future form, it calls for a new earth and a people that do not yet exist." (Goh, 85) This brings us to the radical idea of the *a venir*, or the to-come, a community to come or the philosophical anti-community that auto-rejects all given notions of the community to arrive at the futural contours of the *community to come*. The existing templates of community represent the discursive practices of the establishment and becomes State-capital-community and the rigidities of that community is disarticulated through the Deleuzean idea of the nomadic war machine. Deleuze and Guattari call that the "n-1 community" where the "fragmenting -1 [is] resisting, rejecting, dispersing, or walking away from any form of quantitative and formal totality... that refuses to enter into an economy of the counted in homogenizing structures such as conventional communities." (Goh, 93)

Derridean *Khora*, the Post-Secular Animal-Other and Post-Anthropocentrism

Having traced the *reject* in contemporary French theorization of community and love, Irving Goh then moves to see how French radical thinkers also problematise the question of religion and here too, Goh contextualizes the *reject* within the debates on the postsecular and the postanthropocentric. Derrida in his *Acts of Religion* sees no future for religion if religion "holds on to the phantasm of its sovereign ipseity. That means, Derrida insists on auto-rejection in religion, an auto-rejection that always opens to the other." (Goh, 126) Derrida's naming of ideas such as "messianicity without messianism", or his notion of the "khora" also borders onto the auto-reject in religion. For Derrida

> khora can never be defined, determined, or identified as this or that place. Khora rejects locating itself ... it is no place or nonplace, it is almost an impossible place, yet always necessary to claim proximity to it, or an approximation of it, in order to give voice or place to the new. (Goh, 130)

This impossible but necessary place takes on a clearer contour of a *reject* or the *auto-reject*. For a future thinking of ontology, one must reject any adherence to a particular institution or ground, one must own up the *khora*, the non-ground. If one looks for escaping the postsecular violence of religious and social fundamentalism, then one needs to step further and think of going beyond (auto-rejecting) our anthropocentric or anthropomorphic aspects, a project that incorporates non-human animals, their voices and silences. The existing postsecular discursive practices ignore the consideration of the animals and hence the denial of animals as the "subject of enunciation" should form the subsequent quest for critical theory. If the *khora* allows the "impossible possibility" of the arrival of the other, then we can think of the animal-other, the absolute alterity, or as Derrida called it, the "divinanimality" that "breaks with [...] the similar, to situate oneself at least in a place of alterity radical enough whereby one must break with all identification with an image of oneself, ... with all humanity." (Goh, 136) So the *auto-reject* for the postsecular must follow after the animal. It is "only then that the reject or auto-reject can open religion and/or the postsecular to a future where differences not only between anthropocentric and anthropomorphic religions and reason, but also between humans and animals, are affirmed and respected." (Goh, 138) In this context, Helen Cixous` notion of the "counter Bible" or the animal perspective or the "animots" seem highly relevant. Such animotisation would be our "second innocence" animating divine *jouissance*. Can we then think of a future discourse of politics centering on the non-human or the animal? The idea of "Reject Politics" promoted by Goh marvelously deepens this idea of "becoming non-human", or the "becoming animal" as explicated by Deleuze. At this point, radical possibilities of the *auto-reject* crop up through the inauguration of new notions of the "sans part" as theorised by Ranciere which means the "part that has no part" (Goh, 168). Those who are non-existent in the eyes of the state, the "sans parts" can become the new subject of the *auto-reject*. Ranciere's "sans part" and Baliber's "*maletre*" or "mis-beings" are similar and clamour for "equaliberty" for the "citizen subject" of our society. However both Ranciere and Baliber speak within the framework of the subject and fail to auto-deconstruct their notions of agency and therefore, Goh prefers Derrida's "voyous" or the "rogue-being" as more radical in this respect. The *rogue* is also a figure of the *reject* and in view of Derrida, democratic practices so far, while seeking to "offer hospitality to all the excluded," have paradoxically excluded in particular bad citizens—rogues, non-citizens, and all sorts of dissimilar and unrecognizable others. Welcoming the *voyou*, which is a gesture akin to "unconditional hospitality" may pave the way towards a *democratie a venir*." (Goh, 187) The *rogue being* has "counter-sovereignty" that defies the sovereignty of the state and constitutes "the *voyoucratie*"—a counter power of subversion or anarchy to dismantle the coercive state or absolutist human hegemony. All these posit a critical refusal or the *auto-reject* of existing forms which would enable the impossible possibility of radical democracy which for Derrida is the political experience of the impossible or the political experience of "opening to the other as the possibility of the impossible." (Goh, 196) This impossible figure, in Goh's belief can be the animal, as the animal has always been rejected as a possible figure of thought in politics or political philosophy. To make amends, Goh proposes Deleuze and Guattari's idea of the "becoming animal" which proves itself to be more *voyou* than Derrida's "animal *voyou*", especially in the context of post-anthropocentric geo-politics. Like Derrida, for Deleuze and Guattari too

> there is a politics of becoming animal: To the inhumanness of the diabolical powers` responds the sub human ... of becoming animal: become beetle, become dog, become ape, head over heels and away, rather than lower one's head and remain a bureaucrat... judge or be judged." (Goh, 198)

According to Deleuze and Guattari, "we lack resistance to the present" and Goh would add, "Becoming-animal is that trajectory of resistance, if not force of rejection that we need today". (Goh, 202) In other words, *becoming animal* can resist or sidestep the force of the "state war machine" and hence lead us out of the impasse of contemporary radical political thought. To adopt the idea of *becoming animal* we need to "push existing political thought beyond its anthropologic and/or anthropocentric limits. One must be in fact prepared to even depart from existing models of political thought, rather than to assimilate or even tame becoming animal within their norms." (Goh, 202-203)

Goh would prescribe here the politics of traversal that crosses over to the "animal space". Animal spaces largely escape the gaze and capture of politics and by recovering that very space of exclusion, which the animal occupies after it has been left aside by the frames of normative politics, critical thought can gather a space to slide into and sidestep state politics. In the face of politics of identifiability, "becoming animal" surreptitiously contest the demand for a totalizing coming to presence and presents a haziness before all gazes of the state apparatus. This "disappearance of the "I" is a matter of molecular investment in an animal affect or to molecular politics or revolutionary micro-political action." (Goh, 205) Such a politics, according to Deleuze and Guattari, "resists any apparatus that attempts to delimit a body to a singular entity ... determined by that apparatus". (Goh, 205)

The particular feeling or sensation of animal affects may perhaps be found in the originary and communicative *aisthesis* that humans and animals share. *Aisthesis*, as Aristotle himself has observed, is the irreducible feeling of pleasure and pain that both humans and animals sense and which enables both humans and animals to immediately communicate a wrong done to them. To cross the adjacent space of the animal is a question of recovering the originary *aisthesis*, that is recovering the sensation of the milieu, of aisthesis that "humans and animals originarily share. Originary aisthesis was lost when Aristotle supplemented it with the anthropocentric logos in his political philosophy." (Goh, 202) Aisthesis in its immediate sensing and communication of pain or wrong done to a human or animal is of political potentiality, that is *aisthesis* in itself is already adequate to demand an addressing of the wrong committed against a human or animal. Aristotle however refused to recognize the political potential of aisthesis. To recover aesthesis, before it is supplemented by a form of logos that has been appropriated by and reduced to the human is not only a way towards the adjacent space of *becoming animal*, but is also an unveiling of *becoming animal's* potentiality for a future political project of justice. "Participating in an affect "that is no longer of words," becoming animal becomes invested in an immanent response, "here and now" in Deleuze and Guattari's words." (207) Such a project of justice certainly departs from "the economy of illocutionary exchanges that sustains the spirit of democratic parliamentary discussion." (Goh, 207) The shift to originary *aisthesis* or the refusal to predicate itself on any logocentric system, gives *becoming animal* a further radical political edge as well. *Becoming animal* can be said to be rejecting bio-politics that regulates life in a hegemonic manner. However *becoming animal* proceeds at the molecular dimension, and hence if there is a magnitude to *becoming animal,* it would be at a level of what Deleuze and Guattari would call an "n-1 degree magnitude". They do not fail to articulate the aesthetic dimension of the aisthesis of *becoming animal* and as they believe, "it is through writing" in the sense of literature such as Kafka's writings or Melville's Moby Dick, "that you become animal" (Goh, 209). So art is the site for Deleuze and Guattari where they locate the emergence of *becoming animal.* Hence *becoming animal's* transversal communication between heterogeneous populations open a body to an unlimited relation with any number of living entities. The *becoming animal* ally with the *anomic* and this alliance with the *anomic* is how *becoming animal* challenges the state's politics of (dis)friendship and builds a tranversal politics of the future. This brings us to posthumanism, to ideas of anthropomorphic others or "earth others", to a "zoo-morphic" paradigms. Posthumanism is akin to auto-rejection and in such auto-rejection, posthumanism must be willing to take the risk of allowing new forms of relations it seeks with the reject other to fall into a state of inoperativity. Her Goh employes Nancy's idea of "inoperative community" that suggests a posthumanism to refrain from totalizing all the *rejects* within its discourse. "Critical anthropomorphism" looks into contemporary French thought's idea of the "*clinamen*" which is clearly evident in the works of Michael Seres, Deleuze and Guattari and Nancy. "Clinamen" is some sort of subtractive thinking as "*clinamen* names the process by which atoms detach from a living body or matter without the latter controlling that detachment." (Goh, 233) This is contrary to the accumulative impulse that drives the thought of the human subject, or subjectivity. "In other words, the thought of the *clinamen* takes into account that one is always already in the process of auto-rejecting some part of oneself, even though this takes place at a molecular or atomic scale." (Goh, 233) For a posthumanism that continues the poststructuralist deconstruction of the subject by articulating the *reject*, especially the *reject* that is not borrowed but draws from itself as an *auto-reject, clinamen* can be its point of departure to a world of auto-subtraction/ rejection for multiple dissonances to exist. *Clinamen* and the Deleuzean idea of the *"fold"* render the auto-deconstructive process to usher in infinite incompossibility. From the death of the subject arrives the incompossible genesis of radical post-subjective possibilities. All these radical ontologies point to alternative quest for experimental and fresh insights in unexplored domains of earth study and questions of ethics and subjectivities in the post-Anthpocene age. In what follows I would discuss on how novelties of thought in New Materialist thinking and Critical Animal Studies can also provide those necessary domains of epistemic experimentations.

Conclusion: Towards New Materialism and Critical Animal Studies

I would like to conclude with the findings of New Materialists (Crocket and Robbins) and the proponents of critical animal studies or posthumanist studies through a detour of the works of Matthew Calarco, Stefan Herbrechter and Crockett and Robbins. In their work *Religion, Politics and the Earth: The New Materialism* (2012), Crockett and Robbins defined new materialism as a new discipline that

> takes seriously the material and physical world in which we live. The New Materialism is a materialism based on energy transformation ...For us what we need is a theology that genuinely takes account of the earth without lapsing into wishful thinking about what it means to live in harmony with nature or New Age

platitudes about Gaia that produce a false spirituality. (Crockett and Robbins, 2012, xvi)

Having defined New Materialism, Crockett and Robbins embarked on a wonderful explanation of New Materialist idea of theology, energy, being, politics and ethics. They proposed for an 'athermal idea of energy' keeping in mind the disastrous reality of the Anthropocene and in doing that, unlike Chakrabarty, they launch a severe attack on capitalism and went ahead with a concrete blue print of new politics and ethics which would rally for the hunt for alternative modes of non-heat energy through the application of non-equilibrium thermodynamics. Theirs is a perfect example of cross-disciplinary initiative to stave off the dire consequences of the Anthropocene as they involve a physicist and a radical artist in writing their manifesto on art and energy in the post-Anthropocene. Needless to say such intense and subtle analysis of energy requires specialized knowledge on physics and energy science but credit goes to the New Materialists as they perfectly blends specialized knowhow with a clear proposition for alternative earth centric materialist modes of thinking vis a vis energy, politics and ethics.

> We work against philosophical idealism by taking the earth as subject rather than simply asserting and upholding the vantage point of spirit. Into this Hegelian or quasi Hegelian space, we are also asserting or inserting a Deleuzian emphasis on the earth. In *A Thousand Plateaus*, Deleuze and Guattari ask "Who does the earth think it is?" as they posit not a genealogy of morals a la Nietzsche but a geology of morals—an earth based science of right and wrong, good and evil that not only inspires but also helps to define our project with the new materialism... We posit earth as subject... Earth becomes itself by thinking through its own materiality, energy, forces, layered strata, atmosphere, magnetosphere ... this process is dynamic and entropic process but it relies upon a reconceptualisation of thermodynamics provided in part by Deleuze in *Difference and Repetition*... we claim that energy is immanent Deleuzo-Hegelian spirit (or Spirit), and energy avoids the traditional dichotomy between

> spirit and matter, because everything is energy transformation ... the earth is the solution to the energy crisis, but we do not know how to think like the earth, what Deleuze and Guattari call the mechanosphere. We need to deterritorialize our thinking to unlink it from preestablished ruts and prescribed territories... As such this book is an experiment in thinking. (Crockett & Robbins, xx-xxi)

This is indeed radical stuff and the proposed drive for reterritorialization of our thoughts looks for a carbon free future, or desires to constitute life beyond the paradigm of *Homo Crabonicus* (96), something that the delusion of corporate capitalism has deeply entrenched in our minds about the unending supply of fossil fuel induced energy in this planet. This hunt for the alternative also takes into account the non-human *other* or the animals as they lead their life in consonance with the Earth. The deconstruction of the anthropogenic self would be complete if we pull us down the pedestal of human superiority and critical animal studies as theorized by Matthew Calarco, Cary Wolfe and Paola Cavalieri in their works is another way beyond Anthropocenetric closures.

In works such as *Zoographies: The Question of the Animal from Heidegger to Derrida* (Clarco, 2008), *The Animal That Therefore I Am* (Derrida, 2008); *The Death of the Animal: A Dialogue* (Cavalieri, 2009); *The Animal Question in Deconstruction* (Turner, 2013), *Thinking Through Animals: Identity, Difference and Indistinction* (Calarco, 2015), etc we come across radical possibilities of thoughts through which we auto-reject our anthropogenic pride and self-ordained speciality to accommodate the non-human other. Such reterritorialization of thinking can usher in the ways of new discourses in the aftermath of the Anthropocene. The future of humanities and social sciences will have to traverse through these radical experimentations and deconstructive thinking that toy with ideas of 'divinanimality', 'geology of morals', 'clinamen', 'humanimality', 'zoographies', etc to reduce the disastrous impact of the Anthropocene.

REFERENCES

Archer, David, *The Long Thaw, How Humans are Changing the Next 100,000 Years of Earth's Climate*, NJ, Princeton University Press, 2009.

Calarco, Matthew, *Thinking Through Animals: Identity, Difference, Indistinction*, Stanford University Press, 2015.

Calarco, Matthew, *Zoographies: The Question of the Animal from Heidegger to Derrida*, Columbia University Press, 2008.

Chakrabarty, Dipesh, "Climate and Capital: On Conjoined Histories", *Critical Inquiry*, Vol. 41, No. 1, Autumn, 2014.

Chakrabarty, Dipesh, "The Climate of History: Four Theses", *Critical Inquiry*, Vol. 35, Winter, 2009.

Crockett, Clayton, Robbins, J., *Religion, Politics and Earth: The New Materialism*, New York, Palgrave Macmillan, 2012.

Derrida, J, *The Animal That Therefore I Am*, New York, Fordham University Press, 2008.

Goh, Irving, *The Reject: Community, Politics and Religion after the Subject*, New York, Fordham University Press, 2015.

Lovelock, James, *The Vanishing Face of Gaia*, New York, Allen Lane, 2009.

Turner, Lynn, *The Animal Question in Deconstruction*, Edinburgh, Edinburgh University Press, 2013.

8

Art as *Dissensual Sensorium*: Subaltern Aesthetics and the Logic of Global Corporate Capital

As self-education art is the formation of a new sensorium—one which signifies, in actuality a new ethos. Taken to an extreme, this means that the 'aesthetic self-education of humanity' will frame a new collective ethos. The politics of aesthetics proves to be the right way to achieve what was pursued in vain by the aesthetics of politics, with its polemical configuration of the common world. (Ranciere, 2010, 119)

Art lives so long as it lives in as much as it is something else than art, namely a belief and a way of life... When art is no more than art, it vanishes. (Ranciere, 2010, 123)

The very term "biopolitics" implies this constitutive project. In short, when we live under globalization, when we live in a world whose boundaries are insuperable, when the Copernican revolution has definitively exhausted itself and Ptolemy and the centrality of the kairos have become the only reference point, when all this is the case, what does it mean to develop the creative and constitutive spirit of artistic practice?
(Negri, 2007, 55)

When the only possibility for action, artistic and ethical, consists in moving out from within being, through biopolitical practice, such that every making is a transformation of the very physical and spiritual essence of the human body; when the structure of the social has become so central and the world so small and restricted that there is no longer any possibility of

> *leaving this habitat behind, when utopian illusions (illusions of other topoi) no longer present themselves; what, then, does it mean to act artistically? It means constructing new being; it means making global space reflect back on itself, re-directing it towards the existence of singularities. Will this mean acting to eliminate death, to dissolve the internal limits of the global machine? The monster promises us nothing less.*
>
> (Negri, 2007, 55)

This chapter seeks to unpack Jacques Ranciere's hypothesis of a new artistic and political sensorium through a reference to Indian people-art, specifically the wall paintings of Purulia, a tribal populated district in the Indian state of West Bengal. The selection of Purulia as a locale of reference is crucial since it touches upon both the unique artistic ontology and the political sign system of a region which is known in India as a site of fierce anti-corporate-capital political insurgency and singularity of tribal art-world. The *dispositif* of globalization has unleashed an unquestioning hegemon of marketized kitsch culture that nibbles at the very existence of the rich reservoir of people-arts in India and Purulia is no exception. However the tribal multitude in Purulia has scripted a counter narrative of globalized development and homogeneity of culture by adhering to their very own artistic *dasein* and the wall paintings of the tribals in Purulia as well as other performative folk arts in the adjacent areas foster a promise for a new collective ethos of resistance in the face of global cultural onslaughts. In this essay, I plan to explore the constitution of a materialist ontology or a constitutive ontology of dissent through people-art or folk-political in the light of Ranciere's theory of aesthetic politics and Negri's idea of singularity of artistic resistance in the time of empire. The central premise of Ranciere in his theorization on art and politics investigates notions of community and social bondings that arise in the solitude of the art work practiced in the human communes and here I argue that in the visual *dichtung* of tribal wall paintings of Purulia one exactly encounters this solitude of the art work and a sense of community bonding which defy the logic of global corporate capital in the age of Empire. What is transferred in this bond is 'sensation' and Rancière intends to elaborate on how human action is tied together through this sensory 'fabric' that arises from a shared distribution of the sensible; which, to use his words, 'defines their way of being together.' (Ranciere, 2009) A quick glance at some of the tribal wall paintings of Purulia would substantiate this notion of an artistic sensorium that constitutes a singular aesthetico-political ontology of resistance. Apart from Ranciere, I also draw upon Antonio Negri's conceptualization of art and multitude in the age of Empire as new subjectivities. When the topoi of a constitutive utopia look retreating, Negri would argue for forging the contours of new beings and new singularities through art and this essay seeks to probe, in the light of Negrian analysis, into the immanent and constituent potential of people-art that can unleash an antagonistic praxis of self-liberation or can coronate the sovereignty of the social collective capable of composing a coherent project of revolutionary transformation in the age of global capital. I propose to enquire if people-art can be seen as the Spinozian manifestation of *potentia* (constituent power) or Potenza (living labor) articulating the desires of the multiplicity of human singularities or *multitudo* whose collective power produces the world of counter power. Drawing on Antonio Negri's idea of the *conatas* or *kairo* and Jacques Ranciere's conceptualization of aesthetic politics which suggests a foundational drive for subjectivity or a new temporality of *vis viva* or mutating constituent power of living creative labor, I wish to see if people-art can be liberated from epistemic subjugation and academic neglect by foregrounding their singular power to forge a new plank of aesthetic sensorium, a new domain of artistic metaphysics which helps in launching a counter-hegemonic historiography to reinstate the small voices of history, voices that attends to the pre-colonial idea of the *Gemeinschaft* or community that undo the univocity of the current globalised elitist sign system. Along with these two continental thinkers (Ranciere and Negri), recent works of Gayatri Chakravorty Spivak, a key figure in postcolonial critical scholarship has also reinforced the logic of constituting a counter-logic of hegemony by exploring the construction of new collectivities and newer agents of aesthetic/artistic epistemology. The first paragraph of Spivak's Introduction to her recent book, *An Aesthetic Education in the Era of Globalizaton* announces, 'Globalization takes place only in capital and data. Everything else is damage control.' (Spivak, 2012) According to Spivak, the 'most pernicious presupposition today is that globalization has happily happened in every aspect of our lives,' yet, she objects, it 'can never happen to the sensory equipment of the experiencing being' in any significant way. It is this 'experiencing being', the part of us that can learn to recognize and to swerve from the beliefs and desires of globalization that Spivak addresses in her new book. For Spivak, the new, electronically homogenized and all-pervasive information flow which is adapted to and created by a desire to attach oneself to the flashy powers of capital and data have ruined, among other things, "knowledge and reading." The effect of this is that most of us no longer know what to do with the information to which we are exposed. Information is now most often sorted but not analyzed in any depth; it is used mostly to support the new globalized electronic capitalist model. When scholars in the humanities try to join the globalization parade, the result is that they become 'epistemologically challenged market analysts,' and are 'no longer a moving epistemological force.' They will increasingly be like 'the opera, serving a peripheral function in society.' Spivak advocates a return to an earlier model of reading and of knowledge formation, one that embraces intellectual wandering and chance and avoids limiting itself to the rational and to self-interest. In that spirit, Spivak offers her new hypothesis which, as she tells us, concern itself with a "productive undoing" of the current popular aesthetic of what should be learned and desired. She strives to alter the aesthetic—that which forms the premises of 'the doing' beneath the globalization—by looking carefully at 'the fault lines of the doing . . . with a view to use.' The goal of Spivak's approach is to create a new aesthetic basis, one with different premises, from which a new epistemology could develop, one that will promote the emergence of new—and ideally less destructive and numbing—desires. Spivak sees hope for aesthetic education in the subaltern, a hope that some sympathetic intellectuals and social mobilisers still believe they can learn from those below. She explicitly denies that she is advocating or 'romanticizing the aboriginal'; rather, this would be taking from the subaltern a view of the world not dependent on reason and self-interest. 'We want to open our minds to being haunted by the aboriginal. We want the spectral to haunt the calculus.' The new aesthetic / political epistemology derived from the subaltern, from the margin, from the non-global market calculus life-world, I believe, can inspire a restoration of people-art as the new domain of artivism or the spectral or the new aesthetic tool of 'productive undoing' of the hegemonic. Any functional change in the sign system, Spivak reminds us 'is a violent event' (Spivak, 1985, 331) with huge political reversal effect, turning things upside down and this alteration in the signification system supplements a lack or void in the signified. Echoing Spivak, I may add that by anointing people-art or any existing folk political forms as potential subjectivity one can supplement the lack in the existing master signifiers of epistemic practices. Such a reversal or theoretic tremor would revise all existing concept metaphors, bringing hegemonic historiographies and cognitivities into crisis. The entire socius, Spivak reminds us (and her valued observation appears more true in today's context) is 'what Nietzsche would call a *fortgesetzte Zeichenkette*—a continuous sign chain' and the 'possibility of action lies in the dynamics of the disruption of this object, the breaking and relinking of this chain' (Spivak, 1985, 332). Such a vision enables the ethics of resistance to be inserted into the sign system of bourgeoisie politics and as the sophisticated vocabulary of academic theory and elitism shields their 'cognitive failure' to read the signs of contemporary domination, the necessity to constitute a grammar of radical supplementarity becomes all the more important to undo all forms of theoretic metalepsis that fails to assert any progressivist taxonomy of neo-subjectivity. The existing theoretic metalepsis causes our inability to see the new subject as the subaltern and this negation or failure led to the emptying of the subject. The epistemic violence that led to the effacement of the subject that was obliged to cathect (occupy in response to a desire) the space of the other can be strategically reverted through the reinscription of subaltern/ subject consciousness. Subaltern consciousness as emergent collectivity may help in composing the prose of counter-insurgency and the semiotropy of these aesthetic small voices of history can be construed as a rebel consciousness akin to Marx's idea of 'un-alienated practice' or Gramsci's notion of an ideologically coherent, spontaneous philosophy of the multitude' (Spivak, 1985, 342). The present article makes a case for people-art as a political ensemble or as a site of the people nation that locates the agency of dissent within the narrative of the marginalized multitude. In the subsequent section I will see how such political artivism or the new Negrian idea of multitude can promote a theoretic plexus for dissent and antagonism, categories highly in demand to dissipate the univalence of global capitalist order.

Productive Undoing of Market Calculus Through Art

Spivak is clearly in favour of foregrounding marginal epistemes like folk art, tribal cognitivities to subvert the calculative diorama of globalized capital. She is for retrieving the primordial experience Being through a sustained logic of alternative subaltern subjectivity and in this section I will supplement the Spivakian hypothesis with Negri's idea of the multitude undoing the unitary logic of global capital. In the

Negrian concept metaphor, art unhinges every precept; every prefiguration; and also every unitary matrix, whether spatial or temporal; and it's in the midst of Being, that a convulsive creativity takes hold, not genealogies of vanguards, but the concrete history of multitudes of singularities. For Negri, post-globalization, the world has become both enormous and very small and in the global financescape, there is no longer any God. The space is smooth and superficial; the immanence of value entrusts itself only to the works of men. What does it mean to be an artist in this situation? Every time 'the limit is reached (and it's a limit without a beyond, one that cannot be surpassed), we cannot but redirect our attention onto the present *kairos*... But what is the *kairos*? In Greek culture it was the moment in time marked by the flight of the arrow: that was a civilization that still envisioned a future, and hence a relationship between releasing the arrow and seeing it to arrive. The arrow launched into the sky could reach the stars. Here, however, the *kairos* is the arrow that strikes our own heart, the arrow that returns from the stellar limit. *Kairos* is the necessity (but also the possibility) of taking ourselves as the starting point of a creative project' (Negri, 2007). According to Negri, it's the possibility of engaging in politics by leading all the elements of life back to a poetic reconstruction. The global world as we know it, as Empire presents it to us in the political order, is a closed world, subject to the entropy that results when space and time have been exhausted. But the multitude that acts within this closed world has learned to transform it, by passing through each subject and towards each singularity making up the world. Negri refers to Foucault who argued that when we thought that history was over, we find it renewing itself on the vertical axis that we are. That is what's happening to us, as multitude and multitudinous body.' This, it seems to Negri, is the meaning of art in the age of Empire and during the time of the multitudes (Negri, 2007, 55). I will argue that the tribal wall paintings of Purulia and other performing arts of adjacent areas in rural Bengal/

India poetically reconstruct the *dasein* of the everyday that desecrates the banal entropy of global capital. Situated within the all-devouring hegemon of global kitsch, the folk arts of Purulia and other adjacent areas have succeeded in retaining the creative convolution of a new aesthetico-political kairos, a political imaginary that has galvanized them in anti-global dissent. Negri's idea of the multitude dissenting against the univalence of global capital is not a far cry from Ranciere's theorization of artistic dissensus, or a new form of aesthetic politics and in what follows I would engage with Ranciere's notion of dissensual art as a mode of new political imaginary or emancipatory episteme and subsequently I will show how the tribal wall paintings of Purulia sustains the possibility of this new episteme that is premised on the ontology of the everyday and subaltern subjectivity.

Dissensus and the Politics of Aesthetics

Ranciere's argumentation on art as a new form of the political have significant impact on the futural possibilities of political and critical configurations and his concept of art and aesthetics as a new sensorium of politics provides grounds for a politics of dissensus amidst global discourse of coercive ideological consensus. In his *The Politics of Aesthetics,* Rancière argued that we need to rethink aesthetics as 'the invention of new forms of life' (Ranciere, 2006, 25). Politics is itself aesthetic in that it requires a sharing of sense in common; art is not the exemplary site of sensory pleasure or the sublime but a critical break with common sense, opening up possibilities of new commonalities of sense. Art as politics is thus a manifestation of what Rancière calls dissensus, or a gap in the sensible itself. Rethinking the avant-garde as 'the aesthetic anticipation of the future,' (Ranciere, 2006, 29) Rancière calls for an aesthetic concerned with 'the invention of sensible forms and material structures for a life to come'. In Rancière's thinking, 'aesthetics of politics,' is a 'politics of aesthetics' itself. We can ascribe this trope of aesthetics of politics to Rancière's tripartite schema of art 'regimes.' Ranciere classified the regimes in three categories and first comes the 'ethical regime of art,' in which artistic images are evaluated in terms of their utility to society. Here, Rancière refers to Plato's banishment of painters from his ideal community. Rancière associates this 'regime' with the antique idea that defines artwork as common craft of labor. Under this regime, he writes, 'the mimetician provides a public stage for the 'private' principle of work' (Ranciere, 2006, 43)—that is, artists' work cannot be granted too much power or acclaim because the laborer performing the 'artistic' task of imitating reality operates according to the same criteria as someone making a bucket, and in this aristocratic way of thinking, common laborers have no voice within society. After the ethical regime comes the 'representational regime of art'. Here, Art 'ceases to be a simulacrum ... and the art of imitations is able to inscribe its specific hierarchies and exclusions in the major distribution of the liberal arts and the mechanical arts.' Art is granted its own sphere with its own rules, and elevated above those of common craft. Politically, this second way of thinking about art objects corresponds to the bourgeoisification of the artist, who is transformed into a figure with his own freedom and independence, elevated above the demands of common labor. The 'aesthetic regime of art,' as envisioned by Ranciere breaks down the various hierarchies of the other regimes, asserting 'the absolute singularity of art and, at the same time, destroy[ing] any pragmatic criterion for isolating this singularity. It simultaneously establishes the autonomy of art and the identity of its forms with the forms that life uses to shape itself.' (Ranciere, 2006, 23) Rancière argues that art can still be free of the restrictions of common craft, but it also doesn't have to be shackled to any particular noble content that distinguishes it from everyday life -- prefiguring a progressive equality in its attack on old aesthetic hierarchies. And this is where the 'politics of aesthetics' comes in. Rancière wants to argue that such artistic egalitarianism is analogous to the breaking down of real social and political hierarchies. The tribal wall paintings of Purulia, mentioned earlier illustrate this everyday episteme of non-hierarchy and the rupture in the given aesthetic a priori. Rancière will argue that new kinds of artworks create new communities and ways for people to relate to one another and there cannot be a better example of such new community sense than in tribal art which is worlded in the very soul of bonding and togetherness. For him, this gives them a possible relation to politics. Rancière insists that the 'aesthetic regime' has something liberating about it because it escapes brute political determination. For Ranciere, 'to put it crudely, you cannot lay your hands on capital like you can lay your hands on the written word [or the visual sign] (Ranciere, 2006, 55). It is indeed redeeming to see that no one can take over and redirect the power invested in language and art. This presupposes a modification in the relationship between the circulation of language and the social distribution of bodies, which is not at all in play in simple monetary exchange.' (Ranciere, 2011) But then the commercialization of artistic production has also led to the Bourdieuian coinage of the term 'cultural capital.' However Ranciere would remind us that politics breaks with the sensory self-evidence of the natural order that destines specific individuals and groups to occupy positions to break the status quo. Politics invents new forms of collective enunciations, it reframes the given by inventing new ways of making sense of the sensible. Politics creates new form as it were of dissensual common sense. Such dissensual politics is only possible according to Ranciere through the artistic savoir-faire. A connection between art and politics should be cast in terms of dissensus, the very kernel of the aesthetic regime is that art works can produce effects of dissensus because they are neither sermonizing nor teleological, it rather designates a reframing of the real by generating a new real or a new critical dispositive that denounces the reign of the commodity and its putrid excrements unleashed by global capital. In the subsequent section I will dwell on various forms of Indian folk arts, their survival struggles and their aesthetic and critical appeal.

People-Art, its Crisis and Survival

India, a land of over 2000 ethnic groups, has a wide diversity of visual art forms and every state in India shows a variety of art forms. Most of these art works are produced by certain communities and are often the chief sources of income. Among well-known folk arts of India are, *Warli painting: Pata Chitra(paintings by rural artisans on a piece of cloth or pata) Madhubani Paintings(paintings of mythological figures and stories with beautiful and breathtaking intricacies), Phad paintings, Kalamkari Paintings, etc.* These arts are often referred to as crafts as distinct from fine arts. However often these art forms are done with such finesse and style that many of these are entering the art market with prices that only high quality fine art can command. These art forms have produced artists of individual distinctions and allowed artists to grow individually. However, as the relentless tidal wave of globalization swept across the world in the last two decades, Indian performing arts too were swept, tossed high and hurled down, without many even noticing that some of the great rivers of performing traditions and systems had changed course or, at times, been reined in forcefully. Other than in academic discussions, performing arts in India and its practitioners are today referred to most commonly as being part of the "entertainment industry." This may seem innocuous enough to some of us, but the usage of the term and its passive acceptance in most circles definitely indicate a paradigm shift in the manner in which the arts are viewed by society at large. That today the arts must entertain and amuse in the manner defined by showbiz, and that they must form part of organized industry is the clear and unambiguous message conveyed by this shift. For creators and artistes who, in an ideal world, create art driven by an artistic urge or by that inexplicable creative charge that propels artistes towards their respective forms of expression, this shift from being an individual artiste or part of an artistic community, to being absorbed into or discarded by the politics and commerce of the entertainment industry, has had a far-reaching impact. A closer examination of the global entertainment industry, its mores and terms, would reveal greater details about the changes steered by globalization. Firmly entrenched in the idea of "increasing material wealth" by the opening up of international markets, globalization is unabashed about its obsession with checks, balances, net profits and turnovers. It would, therefore, seem only natural and come as no surprise that even in the area of performing arts, those genres that have a record of yielding attractive enough turnovers and lucrative profit margins would be easily and successfully globalized. But the wall paintings of Purulia and many such examples of folk art across India have defied this market maneuvering by remaining insular, retaining their own space, the space of the non-capital and the new domain of aesthetic politics must engage with such forms of arts which are practiced by non-descript village women during festival seasons and who live their art in their everyday existence, untrammeled by the discursive epistemic violence of globalization. A cursory glance at the wall paintings would convince one of their simplicity and difference, a stepping back from the sense of the market. The wall paintings articulate a zeitgeist of non-productionist metaphysics, driving home the other voice, may be the third space/voice of enunciation. The motifs of the paintings are drawn from the everyday and the familiar and yet they have achieved the rarefied space of non-reductivity. The wall paintings are sustained by the Heideggerian sense of worldedness, very much embedded within the ontological *dasein* of the tribals and cannot be disentangled into a different realm of ulterior signification. The paintings in fact cease to be paintings, oozing out rather from the very ground of their everyday existence, manifesting the inner crust of their being. This idea of embeddedness/worldedness is alien to the principal logic of global capital which extract everything in terms of its commodity value. The idea of 'culture' is ontologically relational. The ways people eat, dress or lodges, at the different levels of that society are never a matter of indifference says Fernand Braudel in *Civilization Materielle* (Braudel, 1982). Human activities which are deemed as 'superior' by the so-called responsible, gentlemanly urban-metropolitan audience such as dreaming, art, nostalgia and theology relentlessly depreciate the everyday. When subtracted from the totality of human experience then those abstract activities that seek transcendence, end up embracing the market calculus. Folk life generally goes on in the everyday. Ultimately, we the urban population remains the prisoners of our own stereotypes, of the presuppositions of our own social locations when we relate ourselves to folk culture. We are invariably drawn towards elements of local and folk cultures which are only intelligible to our own cultural lenses. There are 'becomings', says Gilles Deleuze, such as actions, perceptions, variations and so on from this flux of becomings we perceive and/or organize beings. Organizing the 'being' out of becomings invariably involves an arbitrary history of conscious choice: that is, accepting what the subject is willing to accept; rejecting what it finds redundant or deleterious to self-interest. In this regard, the 'everyday' as an object of critical thought is difficult to discover. It is difficult because at each moment of its becoming, it escapes our attempt to comprehend it. It goes on, around the clock, over the year in the lives of the people. It repeats itself in the same monotony of routine. Yet it is the everydayness of peoples' lives which constitutes their being, forms their existence and in a way shaping the local and the folk. By virtue of its untranslatability into verbal or visual media, the folk culture resists appearance. Yet, at the depths of life it continues anonymously. It moves on in the same rhythm of continuities and make up the material civilization of the rural spaces and its inhabitants. The food the village people eat, the clothes they wear, the slang they use, the beds on which they lie, the anxieties they share, the pets they have, the fears they hide, the spices they use—all form their quotidian existence. Ranciere, Negri and Spivak would wonder why didn't we look into these marks of the quotidian instead of consciously looking for the effects of globalization and consumerism in rural India? Are we trying to draw a hierarchy between the happening and the non-happening, the active and the dormant, the occasional and the everyday by placing the 'everyday' in a disprivileged location? The 'everyday' creates in a very crucial and significant way the character of the folk life. The totalizing, all-encompassing gaze of the globalized popular culture orders the rural-space in a rational and calculated way and the institutions of the state fix the village, through the technologies of surveillance and discipline, into a frozen and systematic space (Soja, 1997). But the 'everyday' resists the capital's organization of space. It slips into frantic movements, unnoticeable corners and forbidden pockets to challenge the regularity of the capital's space. It brings into being a different space (Islam, 2006). This space is the space of marginal farmers, small peasants and landless agricultural workers and laborers and when we look into the textures of the tribal wall paintings, we encounter the triumph of this every day, the quotidian, the dissensus of a different sensorium amidst the hegemon of capitalist logic. This whole issue of artistic dissent or art's struggle to defy the coercive sign system of global capital is exemplary of the sad fate of art in our current social order. On the one hand, art is seen as one of democracy's most essential pillars: it is the space par excellence for the free expression of ideas, the experimentation with new models of society and yet on the other one encounters gross commercialisation of art to hijack its subversive potential. Needless to say, such reasoning could not be further removed from democratic politics proper, which, according to Jacques Rancière precisely takes place when somebody strives to retains one's own space and own identity which is denied to him/her. It is precisely this 'stepping out of line' that is foreclosed in globalisation which fosters the ideology of sticking to a strongly hierarchized image of society in which politics is regarded as a specialized field of expertise populated by political professionals who are the sole masters of the art of politics. But the subaltern form of retention, the alternative credo of retaining one's own space in the exercise of artistic practices of tribals defy in their own way the *dispositif* of global capital.

Conclusion

According to Bourdieu, the rapid proliferation of neo-liberal ideology in all realms of the lived world would have to be countered by the fierce determination of critical networks 'in which Specific intellectuals '(in the Foucauldian sense of skilled and competent scholars) coalesce as a truly collective intellectual who is able to direct his thoughts and actions independently, who, in short, maintains his autonomy'. (Bourdieu, 2001, 36) In particular, the kind of academia that strictly subscribes to the Anglo Saxon academic tradition of differentiating between scholarship (academic respectability) and commitment (political dedication) can only help the neo liberal breakthrough with its research and insights. Now would be the time to give up academic restraint and re-conquer the political and social sovereignty of interpretation. The 'collective intellectual' would first have to take on negative responsibilities, i.e. to radically criticise the hegemony of the economic over the political and cultural, before contributing to political renewal in a positive way. What is necessary is an alliance for action endowed with the authority of a competent and skilled collective embracing academic disciplines and art communities that implements its critique of the neo-liberal order in the form of direct interventions in the sense of a new agitprop. Where academic, artistic and political practices appear in union, an actual perspective of political participation emerges. For Ranciere the new poetics or the new aesthetic politics frames a new hermeneutics, taking upon itself the task of making society conscious of its own secrets, by leaving the noisy stage of political claims and doctrines and delving to the depths of the social, to disclose the enigmas and fantasies hidden in the intimate realities of everyday life. (Ranciere, 2010, 119)

REFERENCES

Braudel, F., *Civilization Materielle*. London: Collins, 1982.

Bourdieu, Pierre, *Gegenfeuer 2*, Konstanz: UVK, 2001, p.36.

Maidul Islam, "Postmodernized Cultural Globalisation: Threatening Folk Culture(s)", *Social Scientist*, Vol. 34, No. 9/10 (September—October, 2006), pp. 48-71

Negri, Antonio and Max Henninger, *Art and Culture in the Age of Empire and the Time of the Multitudes*, Reviewed, *SubStance*, Vol. 36, No. 1, Issue 112: (2007), 55.

Rancière, Jacques, *The Politics of Aesthetics*, Continuum, 2006, p. 25.

Rancière, J., "Politics, Art & Sense", *Transformations*, Issue No. 19, 2011.

Rancier, J, *Dissensus on Politics and Aesthetics*, London, Continuum, 2010, p. 119.

Rancière, Jacques, *The Emancipated Spectator*, translated by Gregory Elliott (2009), London: Verso, Review by Matt Rodda, *Art & Research: A Journal of Ideas, Contexts and Methods*. Vol. 3. No. 1. Winter 2009/10.

Spivak, Gayatri Chakravorty, *An Aesthetic Education in the Era of Globalization* Cambridge, Harvard University Press, 2012.

Spivak, Gayatri Chakravorty, "Deconstructive Study of History" *in Subaltern Studies, Vol. 4, Delhi, Oxford University Press,* 1985, p. 331.

Soja E. W., *Postmodern Geographies, Re-assertion of Space in Critical Social Theory*, New Delhi: Rawat Publications, 1997.

9

Flawed Postcolonial Historiography?: Subaltern Theory After the *Chibber-Chatterjee Debate*

The present excursus is in response to Partha Chatterjee's rejoinder to Vivek Chibber's recent book, *Postcolonial Theory and the Specter of Capital* (2013), a work that by some accounts "may amount to the most substantive effort to dismantle the field [subaltern theory] through historical reasoning published to date" (Watson, 2013) and also hailed as "an important and timely intervention in the domain of postcolonial theorization that offers the most comprehensive critique to date of subaltern theory" (Purakayastha, 2014) where Chibber has taken both Chatterjee and the other proponents of the Subaltern Studies group to task for what he considers, their flawed and misplaced historical assumptions over which they clustered around their entire theorization of subaltern historiography. Chibber's trenchant critique of the Subaltern Collective's theoretic apercus has already elicited strong counter reactions from Partha Chatterjee during the 2013 Historical Materialism Conference held in New York University and scholars loyal to the subaltern collective would believe that Chatterjee has given a fitting rebuttal to Chibber's arguments and therefore the entire thesis of Chibber's book was found wanting (Nigam, 2013). Since then Chatterjee has published the written version of his debate with Chibber in New York in the celebrated Indian journal *Economic and Political Weekly* (EPW, Vol, XLVIII, No.37, 2013) and the present essay seeks to engage with that response of Chatterjee to investigate the nuances and veracities of this important debate which may decide the futural directions of postcolonial theory. As mentioned earlier, the *Chatterjee Chibber Debate* had an animated fall out in social networking sites and blogs but I would argue that in the light of recent theoretic interventions on postcolonialism, the *Chatterjee Chibber Debate* should be engaged with greater academic sincerity for futural epistemic reformulations. I intend to critically intervene here in this debate and my argumentations would thoroughly engage both Chibber's book and Chatterjee's response to it. At the outset, I would clarify that this is neither going to be a whole hearted advocacy of Chibber's logic nor would it be a substantiation of Chatterjee's positions, on the contrary, I would closely read both to foreground areas for future debates and emergent theoretic cartographies. A rigorous textual analysis of both Chibber's book and Chatterjee's rejoinder reveals that Chatterjee has been largely selective in answering Chibber and has curiously left many questions, raised by Chibber, unanswered. It also appears that Chatterjee perhaps was over swayed by a moderate sense of vengeance in answering Chibber's points. On occasions, when scholars of postcolonialism expect Chatterjee to counter Chibber on questions of *universal well-being* in witty and factual manner, Chatterjee has descended to mere rebukes and invectives. Answering to Chibber's hypothesis of "physical well being" as the criterion for universal class struggle, Chatterjee decides to refute this position as "zoo politics" mockingly suggesting that a concern for physical well-being would drag animals in this discursive fold. This is indeed unbecoming of a towering scholar like Chatterjee and such regressing use of animal metaphors is also bizarre at a time when the global academia is theorizing about the anthropocene (Dipesh Chakrabarty himself has written something on it recently). In what follows, I would first summarize Chibber's contention in his book and then would situate the *Chibber Chatterjee Debate* in the light of this reading so that I can substantiate my argument on Chatterjee's selective rebuttal and his silence over many important areas. On social networking sites and in academic circles in India, Chatterjee's response to Chibber in the New York Historical Materialism debate (the EPW Note is a written version of that debate) has been validated as a triumphant closure of Chibber's critique of Subaltern theory, but I would argue that most of such reactions are not informed by a close reading of Chibber's book or by a critical re-reading of Ranajit Guha's essay "Dominance without Hegemony". My basic contention is Chibber might be over-drawn or harshly sweeping in his dismissal of the Subaltern Collective and some of his conclusions should be challenged, but his book, gifted with a thorough engagement of subaltern theory, undoubtedly has opened up a debate which is crucial in the present conjuncture when one witnesses significant paradigm shifts in the domain of Western theoretic cartography. Post 9/11 theorizations on governance, democracy, state power, citizens` right and global capital and the 2008 economic meltdown induced Occupy movements, the Arab Spring, etc have brought in new and radical theoretic optics and postcolonialism cannot refuse to engage with them. It needs to come out of its old insular stubbornness to arrive at newer theoretic constellations and the *Chatterjee Chibber Debate* has to be located in this backdrop to critically assess its argumentative thematic. Recent scholarship in the field of postcolonialism such as Patrick Chabal's *The End of Conceit: Western Rationality After Postcolonialism* (2013) and Hamid Dabashi's, *The Arab Spring and the End of Postcolonialism* (2013) call for the end of all the ideological productions that we ordinarily identify with the postcolonial period. In the aftermath of European colonialism, the dominant political imaginaries were connected to national sovereignty or postcoloniality and Dabashi identifies three sorts of ideologies that emerged under the postcolonial imaginary, namely, Third World socialism, anticolonial nationalism, and militant Islamism but now these ideologies, as episteme, have arguably exhausted themselves, after the Arab Spring. This new phase has been identified as 'post-Islamism,' or 'post-ideological' and the coming days necessitate new sculptures of thought, or new theoretic repositioning. Both Dabashi and Chabal can be disputed but the bottom line is new configurations of power and new economic realities necessitate new theoretic reframing and in what follows we would closely grapple with the *Chatterjee Chibber debate* to see if new epistemic possibilities can emerge.

Chibber's central concern and findings in his book can be summarized in his own words in the following way—among the claims Chibber encounters and rebuts in Subaltern theory, have been that the Eastern bourgeoisie was not revolutionary, the way the Europeans had been; that it failed to implant liberal institutions, that it continued to rely on political coercion and hence failed to generate bourgeois forms of power; that peasants in the East are not motivated by material interests; that workers are innately religious; and so forth. Because of these deep fissures between East and the West, the theories emerging out of the western experiences are considered to be problematic. In other words, Western theories end up obscuring the real dynamics of Eastern modernity. Hence their (Subaltern School's) rejection of the Enlightenment tradition of Western thought. (210) Chibber in his book, while appreciating the Subaltern Collective for their radical ingenuity and empirical prowess, rebuts these central epistemic premises through a rigorous engagement with three of its central theoretic figures, namely Ranajit Guha, Partha Chatterjee and Dipesh Chakrabarty. So Chibber's project is not a complete dismissal of the Subaltern School because on many occasions in the book he has appreciated their theoretic relevance (157; 166-167; 199). In fact Chibber even praises Chatterjee's ingenuity of analysis and argumentative power and he has also lauded Guha's *Elementary Aspects of Peasant Insurgency* in no uncertain terms, but his central objection has been to register his protest against the Orientalist leanings of the Subaltern Collective who, he believes perpetuates the oriental Other image of the East through their case studies and theorizations and who also missed a great opportunity to what could have been a significant study of class configurations and class struggles in the East.

Universalizing Mission of Capital and *Bhadralok* Historiography: A Flawed Hypothesis

Chibber attempts in his book a theoretic defacement of subaltern historiography as enunciated by Ranajit Guha, Partha Chatterjee, Dipesh Chakrabarty and others by debunking Guha's base line argument of the civilizing mission of the bourgeoisie revolution in Europe as pure illusion and faulty. He slams Guha for mythologizing the people centric orientations of the capitalist revolution in England and in France and he compares Guha's historical conclusions with the Whig traditions of history. Guha traces the root of structural fault between the two modernizing projects—that of Western Europe and of India—in the bourgeoisie's divergent orientation to landed property. Whereas the British and the French elites launched a frontal assault on the feudal nobility, the Indian bourgeoisie, the Subalternists claim, accommodated to it. From these contrasting origins springs the specificity of colonial modernity, a modernity without recognizably capitalist cultural and political forms or so claim the Subalternists. (81) For Chibber, the whole logic of European bourgeoisie striving for capitalist liberalism is blinkered and skewed as historical facts prove otherwise. The European elite did go against the feudal system but they never favoured popular sovereignty. So the whole argument that the Indian bourgeoisie failed to emulate their European counterpart is totally wrong according to Chibber. (82)

Partha Chatterjee in his response to Chibber, speaks of examining Chibber's arguments against the Subaltern Collective whose works, he feels, Chibber has taken rather 'inexactly' to be emblematic of postcolonial theory today. Now this first point is rather intriguing, as the reader is in a fix to know whether this is an indirect admission on Chatterjee's part that the Subaltern School's early works are flawed and therefore have lost their contemporary relevance. Chatterjee accuses Chibber of misreading Guha's positions in his essay, "Dominance without Hegemony" and to explain this, Chatterjee snubs Chibber of foregrounding a "historical sociology of bourgeois revolutions of Europe" which Guha never wanted to focus on and Chatterjee reinforces his point by saying that any reading of Guha's essay would demonstrate that it is meant primarily to debunk colonialist historiography. This is true but Chatterjee, it seems, forgets to address the larger issue Chibber raises in this portion of his book, which is that Guha's central premise in his essay has been *the narrative of the failed universalisation of capital in its colonial journey*. Chatterjee would dismiss this allegation by saying that this point forms a very short portion of Guha's essay, but any reading of the nearly hundred page long essay of Guha would substantiate the flaw in Chatterjee's argument because this logic of capital's universalisation permeates a major chunk of Guha's essay and even if it constitutes a smaller chunk, it cannot take away the counter-argument that Chibber has raised. Chatterjee, it may appear, does not answer Chibber convincingly here.

It is really hard to understand why Chatterjee repetitively resorts to the term "historical sociology" throughout his rejoinder to Chibber. Is it being used as a shield to displace the whole debate in a different direction? Is historical sociology debarred from any scholarly engagement with Subalternism? Besides, what Chatterjee describes as "historical sociology" in fact constitutes the central plank of Chibber's critique of Guha which is that Guha has drawn on some of Marx's flawed notions to conclude the hypothesis of capital's universalisation dynamics. Chibber refers to Marx's sources of bourgeois historiography which valorized the role of liberals in universalizing liberalism through the global march of capital. Here Chibber corrects Marx with strong arguments and added that although Marx borrowed his ideas about capitalism in Europe from bourgeois historiography, he was cautious enough not to be trapped by its liberal and civilizing narratives of universalisation. But when Guha premises his whole argument in his essay on this hypothesis he is completely swayed by this one-sided narrative and hence his logical conclusions too stand open for criticism. Is this historical sociology? Chatterjee's comment, "finally, Guha needs to show that these liberal claims to hegemony for colonial as well as the postcolonial regimes are spurious" seems misleading because a close reading of Guha's essay would say something else. No where do we get a sense that Guha is departing from the colonial narrative of *capital gaining dominance through consent*. He reiterates that what has happened in the West did not happen in India. Therefore, Chatterjee's claim that "He [Guha] needs to make no claims of his own about the real history of bourgeois revolutions in Europe" is also factually incorrect because on numerous occasions, Guha has made such emphatic claims. When Chatterjee in this same context says that Chibber's whole analysis of the class nature of the European bourgeois revolutions which Marx and Guha referred to is beside the point because such analysis "does nothing to Guha's point" he also proves to be wrong. One needs to reread Guha's essay to see the fallacy in Chatterjee's response. As far as Chibber's labeling of Guha's views as a Whig view of history is concerned it has to be understood in the light of the above discussion. What Chibber meant is that the Whigs promoted a romanticized view of capital's liberal history and Guha has consciously or unconsciously fallen a victim of that narrative. So Chatterjee's argument of Guha being against the Whig view of history is true but he fails to answer again Chibber's charge that unknowingly Guha has subscribed to the Whig paradigm when he premises his logic on the universalizing drive of capital. However the greatest misrepresentation of facts by Chatterjee comes when he says,

> In fact, he [Guha] does not anywhere use the term "capitalist" to describe this group [Indian bourgeoisie]. What he means

> is the political intellectual leadership of the liberal nationalist movement... unlike what Chibber surmises, nothing that Guha says about the Indian bourgeoisie is meant to apply specifically to Indian capitalists. (70, EPW)

Now one can safely disagree here, as on several occasions Guha has exactly meant what Chibber signifies. Guha frequently used terms like "heroism of the European Bourgeoisie" (213) and sentences like, "This mediocre liberalism, a caricature of the vigorous democratic culture of the epoch of the rise of the bourgeoisie in the West..."; "how is it that no real effort is ever made by historians on either side to link these paradoxes to any structural fault in the historic project of the bourgeoisie?" (214) Guha indeed talked in great detail about the universalist pretensions of capital in his essay from pages 222-226 and to be fair to Guha he also reminds us of Marx's cautious approach not to be entrapped by this illusion of universalization. The various exceptions to this universalizing claim is also documented on page 226 of his essay but it is also true that Guha repeats Marx's belief on many occasions about the comprehensive nature of the French and the English revolution of 1648 where Marx lamented that compared to these two, the German revolution of 1848 was a "mere parody of the French Revolution of 1789."(227) Guha also mentioned the "vigour" and "decisiveness" of the French bourgeoisie in their struggle against feudalism (227) and one must understand that Chibber raises his objection to this reiterated foregrounding of the French Revolution as totally pro-people. Guha quotes Marx when the latter said

> ... The French bourgeoisie of 1789 never left its allies, the peasants, in the lurch. It knew that the abolition of feudalism in the countryside and the creation of a free, landowning peasant class was the basis of its rule... (227)

Guha uses this statement of Marx to criticize other bourgeois revolutions which failed to emulate the French and English revolutionary standards as highly relevant to study colonialism, "the relevance of this critique for the study of colonialism can hardly be overestimated."(227) Guha calls for "situating [oneself] outside the universe of liberal discourse"(229) while scripting historiography of colonial India, but the question remains whether his basic premise about the failed career of capital in its universalization drive in the East itself is sustained by this liberal discourse.

Guha dwelt on the organic composition of colonial dominance and native subjugation (D/S) at great length in his essay and came out with various forms of coercive mechanisms the state employed to attain forced consent. Coercion was part of colonial governance and Guha repeats the "paradoxes" of colonialism which retained pre-capitalist practices in India, in fact such practices, Guha says, were reinforced under colonial rule in India. The native pre-colonial notions of penology such as *Danda and Dharma/Raj Dharma* as laid down in *Manu Samhita* were appropriated by the British to exercise their dominance (D) over religiously governed natives. While talking about the concept of *Improvement* and *Dharma*, Guha discussed the *idiom of improvement* which colonialist historiography used to promote the liberal character of the raj and here too Guha maintained that such liberal character "was the cardinal feature of the political culture of England for the greater part of a century beginning with the 1780s."(240) This narrative of improvement was a strategy to achieve collaborative help from the propertied class or the indigenous elite and such vocabularies of improvement or pro-people stance gained ground, Guha said because of the *Dharmic* notions of politics in India and this *Dharmic* political optic prevented any acknowledgement of class struggle in Indian politics. This local ingredient in Indian politics was also coupled with the cult of *bhakti* or obedience/duty where the notion of right based politics had no place. As a result, Guha says, "the colonial subject constitutes himself in a loyalist discourse."(254) This overwhelming presence of *bhakti* generated a servile or "*dasyam-manyatvam*"(257) tendency among the subjugated subjects who were tutored to be servile to the king as they are to the deity and this sense of servility or passivity caused continued subordination and Guha locates the dynamics of D/S within the religious sentiments of colonial India. Guha asserts, "There is nothing in the nature of authority in precolonial India which is not comprehensively covered by these three dyads—*Palaka/Palya, Prabhu/Dasa and Lalaka/Lalya.* (260) In other words, one witnesses the "constitutionalism of *rajbhakti*" in colonial India. But Chibber would rightly ask, is it only true for India? Was not the royalty in England treated as a God too? From page 240 to page 272, Guha elaborated on the idea of religious cults and *Dharmic* protest in Indian society and explained the absence of right based politics in India because of the pervasive presence of *dharma* in Indian psyche. However one fails to understand when Guha reads the peasant insurgencies in Bengal as modes of *dharmic* protest, which elites like Bankim Chandra could not comprehend as he was schooled in the liberal mode of thinking but the question remains, if the entire national political spectrum was marked by *dharmic* protests, then how did the subaltern protest emerge? Guha went on chronicling the co-existence of two paradigms in colonial India which constituted the central paradox of Indian politics under colonial rule and Guha raises some questions here which I think is highly important in the context of the *Chibber-Chatterjee Debate*. Guha asks,

> Why did the establishment of British paramountcy over the subcontinent fail to overcome the resistance of indigenous Indian culture to the point of being forced into a symbiosis? Why did the universalist drive of the world's most advanced capitalist culture, a phenomenon that corresponded to the universalizing tendency of the of the most dynamic capital of the time, fail, in the Indian instance, to match the strength... of its political dominion over a subject people by assimilating, if not abolishing, the pre-capitalist culture of the latter? For it is the drive which as Marx argues in The German Ideology, makes the emergence of 'ruling ideas', a necessary concomitant of capital's dominance in the mode of production, and it is precisely these 'ruling ideas' which assign

> to the bourgeoisie the historic responsibility to 'represent' the rest of the society, to speak for the nation, and thereby invest itself with hegemony. (273)

If we are to believe this line of thinking then the D/S equation is to be forgotten and this quote of Guha is important because here he seems to be suggesting that the British would treat India as their own country. One also fails to gather from this quotation that it is meant to counter the claims of colonial historiographers. Guha again asks similar questions, "how come that in India universalism failed to generate a hegemonic ruling culture like what it had done at home?" At no time does Guha question the basic premise that the European bourgeoisie restructured social patterns in their home, something that Chibber has called into question. One also finds it difficult to understand when Guha asks

> how is it that even at its hour of triumph the universalist tendency was resigned to live at peace with heterogeneity and particularity of the indigenous political culture of an Asian colony? How come that in India universalism failed to generate a hegemonic ruling culture like what it had done at home? (274)

Did Marx mean homogeneous behavior of capital both in normal and in colonial conditions? So the *decalage* of the "most dynamic power of the contemporary world" inserting into the structure of a pre-capitalist feudal culture and therefore regressing from its universalist drive is perhaps not a compromise but something expected from a colonialist power hell bent on usurping the subjugated and when Guha says, "an unconscious tool of history" had obviously lost its edge and was consigned by history to the company of other blunt instruments in its bottom drawer"(274), he is perhaps assigning the British, like the colonialist historiographer, whom he attempts to mock, a bigger role than the philanthrophist. If we listen to Guha again the fault lines get clearer,

> its[colonial paradox] effect on the organic composition D was to undermine the magnitude of P[persuasion] in relation to that of

> C[coercion] within the moment of colonialism. In other words, D as a term of the central relation of power in the subcontinent, meant dominance without hegemony. The Prince who, on the Centaur's advice, had so deftly balanced the beastly and the humane in politics for over four centuries, appears to have lost his touch, and the exercise of authority in realms far from metropolitan Europe came to rely on fear rather than consent. (275)

In this passage, Guha's axiomatic faith in the liberalized narrative of capital in metropolitan Europe is loud and clear and Chibber is exactly pointing at such axioms. Chatterjee however, decides not to say anything on such instances. When we approach such notions of the liberalist Prince's universalisation drive to align the beastly with the humane with contemporary theoretic interventions of *The Beast and the Sovereign (Derrida, 2009), and capital's treatment of "Rogues" states, (Derrida, 2003),* Guha and Chatterjee's claims and expectations from capital appear more naïve. Today's *lyco-politics* of the capitalist world to annihilate the fringe nations in the name of terror and democracy makes the *Chibber Chatterjee debate* more relevant. The despotic and autocratic nature of the Raj is expected from the colonizers and therefore it comes as no surprise that they decided to go for covert and overt forms of coercion in their rule in India. John Locke's theory of social contract should not be expected in a colonial context because had the colonialists followed the Lockean ideals, they would not have annexed India in the first place as a colony and once they have subjugated us, they would justify it by all means as Prospero did in Shakespeare's *Tempest*, but that does not mean that Caliban would wait for Prospero's benevolence to universalize the mission of liberal policies. When Guha says that "bourgeois culture hits its historic limit in colonialism" (277) his entire logic seems to stand on the presumption that colonialists came to India to serve the Indians and therefore his surprise at "how professions of bourgeois democracy were violated in the practice of imperialism" (279) fails to gain much ground. In answering Dodwell's, the colonial historiographer's validation of the British "rule of law" Guha ends up advocating the basic premise of metropolitan bourgeois culture, "nothing could testify more to the failure of metropolitan bourgeois culture to inform the structure of authority in the subcontinental colony fully by its own content."(281) One is really surprised and clueless when Guha laments in his essay,

> ...the same bourgeoisie which, having come of age, had established its hegemonic dominance in metropolitan Europe and expanded into a colonial empire only to realize that its rule over its Asian subjects must rely, alas, more on force than consent. (282)

It is true that colonial historiography contributed as Guha said to the fabrication of the "spurious hegemony" but that is what is expected of it, because this narrative of civility masquerades the mercantilist historiography of the East India Company. Having exposed the collaborational and collusive line of the Cambridge School of history which valorized only elite and organized forms of politics in the form of "horizontal solidarity" opposed to the native form of "vertical solidarity" based subaltern politics, Guha characterized colonial political and historical narrative as "monistic, reductionist tactic to impoverish politics by an arbitrary expurgation of its mass content and by narrowing it down merely to an interaction between the colonizers and a very small minority of the Indian population made up of the elite. It is monistic because it is designed to contain all of politics within a single elitist domain."(305) The penultimate part of the essay subtitled as "Preamble to an Autocritique" as referred to by Chatterjee to refute Chibber's reading of Guha, indeed talks of an autonomous historiography free from the "concave universe of liberal ideology" but in that same section Guha once again asks, "what is there in the power relations of that rule which makes the colonial state in our subcontinent so fundamentally different from its architect, the British metropolitan state?"(308). Is it hard to see the implied axiom of the unquestioned assumption of a liberal metropolitan culture in this differentiation of Guha? In his bid to acquire in his brilliant essay, the "urgency and sanctity of a struggle for expropriating the expropriators", Guha perhaps remained imprisoned to the primary signification of metropolitan supremacy.

Abstract and Concrete Labor

In response to Chibber's analysis of Marx's notion of abstract labor, Chatterjee says that Dipesh Chakrabarty derived his universalizing tendency of capital from Marx's analysis of the logic of capitalist accumulation and capital in India encountered social forms of existence of labor that it could not transform into homogeneous labor. Industrial production under colonial conditions thus posed according to Chakrabarty, an obstacle to the universalizing tendency of capital. Chatterjee rebukes Chibber for saying that "what is universalized under the rule of capital... [are] the compulsions of market dependence."(125). Chatterjee finds it hard to understand how market dependence alone can be a sufficient criterion for the universalisation of capital. But is Chatterjee being selective here in quoting Chibber? In fact Chibber has said a lot in the book on this question of abstract labor. Chatterjee went on to say that while Chakrabarty premised his arguments on Marx's definition of abstract labor, Chibber has decided to reject Marx in his enunciation of the same subject. But any reading of Chibber's long sixth chapter would testify that this is perhaps a misrepresentation on Chatterjee's part, because Chibber did not depart from Marx and he devotes this whole chapter to explain his position on abstract labor in the light of Marx. For paucity of space, one cannot quote all those references but having explained his Marxian understanding of abstract labor, Chibber concludes that racial hierarchies, and by extension social hierarchies of the kind that worry Ranajit Guha and Dipesh Chakrabarty are consistent with the dynamics of capitalist accumulation and with the concept of abstract labor.

Chibber therefore, rejects the argument that capital failed to break the heterogeneity of labor into abstract labor in its journey to global south and therefore, in order to theorise the constellation of power in postcolonial nations there is no need to construct new theoretic frameworks. The category of abstract labor, contrary to the arguments of the subaltern school, Chibber believes is perfectly capable to explain the enduring social heterogeneity of the working class. Chibber now debunks the allied argument of the subalternists that democracy arrives through the agency of capital, in other words, no bourgeoisie, no democracy.

Chibber here refers to theorists like, Goran Therborn who argued that "it was the organized working class, not the bourgeoisie that had played the pivotal role in European democratization."(147) In other words, it was a consequence of mass movements that elite political culture and elite institutions were forcibly integrated with those of the laboring classes, forging one integrated sphere. The key to the dissolution of the subaltern domain then was not a bourgeoisie following through on the promises it had made to workers and peasants as it recruited them into its coalition; it was the mobilization of the lower orders, forcing the dominant class to relinquish its monopoly over social and political power. So the key to the emergence of an integrated political order that Ranajit Guha talked about is not the bourgeoisie, but through the consolidated efforts of the subaltern classes. The reason for the political sphere in India not undergoing the sort of integration that the West experienced in its modernization, is the structural, or organizational or even cultural facts about the working class and the peasantry. Then why were they not able to amass the organizational capacity? Were popular alliances in the colonial struggle compromised in some way? Has the postcolonial order somehow diluted class identities? According to Chibber, these are some of the questions that might shed some light on the persistence of popular subordination. But such questions, Chibber alleges, rarely appear in Guha's work and Chatterjee, has not cared to answer any of such questions in his rejoinder. For Chibber, they do not appear because they cannot. Guha cannot ask this question because he mistakenly identifies the bourgeoisie as the pivotal actor in the emergence of non-feudal political modernity. Subaltern studies, Chibber comments, was swept away by cultural theory by not focusing on the Subaltern groups` contribution to break free of the feudal past and

> in making this mistake—attributing the emergence of bourgeois-democratic political formations to the practice of the capitalist class, and insisting that only one form of power can be regarded as capitalist—Guha not only made a colossal scholarly and analytical blunder; he also foreclosed the possibility of a genuine comparative study of the postcolonial world's path to modernity, based on real comparisons instead of the imaginary ones that populate the pages of Subalternist scholarship. (150)

This is a very serious charge and one expected Chatterjee to engage with such questions, but instead of dealing with such theoretic positions, Chatterjee decided to accuse Chibber of forgetting Marx. For Chibber therefore, the Subalternists are wrong when they say that abstract theories cannot apprehend the production of and persistence of social differences. The concept of abstract labour can sustain and even create tremendous diversity in social identities.

Peasant Consciousness, Nation and the Orientalist Optic

After praising Chatterjee for his minute empirical research (166-167), Chibber's take on Chatterjee's study of peasant consciousness in India is, Chatterjee seems to be unaware that

> he is reviving a well-established Orientalist notion of the East as a culture in which actors are essentially other oriented, lacking any notion of individuality, unmoved by their material interests... all this has a drearily familiar ring to it, even if dressed in radical language, for it harks back directly to nineteenth century colonial ideology, not to mention contemporary reifications of

the unchanging East. (160—161)

Chibber reminds us that Chatterjee in fact is going away from Guha in making such claims because "there is little in Guha's *Elementary Aspects of Peasant Insurgency* that warrant Chatterjee's characterization."(162) On the contrary, according to Guha what seems central to peasant consciousness "is not the sense of duty or obligation, but the appreciation of risk, the regards for their interests, and the hesitation to bear the costs of collective action."(162) Guha had in fact shown in his book that insurgent leaders had to resort in many different ways to inducements, exhortations, sanctions and even threats. Hence there is little evidence, Chibber says, that Guha regards solidarity as an elemental pre-given datum of peasant consciousness, or that he sees individual interest as irrelevant to it. In fact Guha's analysis in *Elementary Aspects* simply "joins the pantheon of classics in agrarian studies that confirm the importance of material interests in peasant psychology, both East and West."(166)

Chatterjee, we are told by Chibber, is marked by many contradictions in his theorization of peasant consciousness and various internal differentiation within peasant community belies Chatterjee's claims about the unique "paradigmatic form" of peasant consciousness in India. If individual interest played little role in peasant agency, then peasant acquisition of land, their pursuit of strategies to snatch away their peer's resources, is simply incomprehensible. They on the contrary speak volumes of their materialist nature. In fact Guha and Chatterjee actually furnish us, Chibber argues, with a story in which Indian peasants look very much like peasants everywhere else. It is entirely possible to assimilate the history of Indian peasants into a universal history of the peasantry.

According to the Subaltern School if the historian is to seek out the reasons for the agents` choice of action then they have no alternative but to decode the "internal logic of a culture," since it is this logic that agential reasoning follows. Chibber quotes Chakrabarty,

> unlike in the case of the "citizen", the jute worker's political culture, lacking any bourgeois notions of equality of the individual, had not split him into his "public" and "private" selves; and he had not, unlike the citizen, relegated all "the distinctions based on birth" to the sphere of the "private" ... In this sense, the jute mill worker had never been politically emancipated from religion. Religion, therefore—or we could say, ethnicity, or language or other similar loyalties—formed the staff of his politics. (184)

If this is true then what is the source of its emergence? Surprisingly, after arguing that workers` consciousness could not break out of its prison house, Chakrabarty, Chibber says, simply puts down his pen. He never tells the reader what might be the source of the new culture of rights and equality. (186) Chibber would argue that Jute mill workers in Calcutta carried their traditional norms with them as they made the transition to factory life, just as the migrants from Bihar did when they undertook the journey to Calcutta's jute mills. When they organized their unions, or fought for voting rights, or asked for more congenial working conditions, they did these things while still being steeped in elements of their culture –something which Chakrabarty described as pre-bourgeois. Chibber continues,

> If Chakrabarty and Chatterjee are correct that a prebourgeois consciousness will not countenance any notion of individual interest, then the struggle against bourgeois despotisms in Europe, or slavery in Americas, has to be a modern miracle. European workers were not born into the world holding a copy of *The Rights of Man* in one hand and *The Social Contract* in the other. They were every bit as enveloped in traditional ideology and primordial loyalties as were their Indian counterparts a couple of centuries later. They were no more the secular citizen-subject than were the jute workers in Clacutta. So on what psychological resources did workers or slaves draw upon when they fought against their masters, if they could not understand that their well-being was undermined by their oppression? (204)

Partha Chatterjee again decides to evade such important questions and did not answer this in his rejoinder. While talking about Chatterjee's take on nationalism in works like *The Nation and its Fragments* and *Nationalist Thought and the Colonial World,* Chibber dwells on Chatterjee's accusation of nationalism as something completely wedded to the ideological apparatus of colonial discourse. It is, Chatterjee explains, locked to the narrative of reason and capital. Chatterjee however failed to offer any alternative and Chibber says, "Chatterjee does not offer a strategy for the postcolony because he cannot"(281) Interestingly Chatterjee's critique of nationalism, Chibber quips, sounds like a traditional Marxist critique of elite nationalism and Chatterjee's comment that nationalism was flawed because it never "challenged the legitimacy of the marriage between Raeson and capital"(281) is, Chibber says the only isolated instance of pro-Marxist views which is

> outweighed by the numerous instances, scattered across the book, in which he inveighs against the Enlightenment tradition as a whole, not merely the bourgeois stream within it. He carefully levels his main criticism against the idea of modernization itself, never hinting that he intends to limit his argument to capitalist modernization. (282)

Chatterjee is silent on this too and he is also silent on Chibber's allegation that he (Chatterjee) "never takes up Gandhi's defense of the propertied classes, his ambivalence towards trade unions, his philosophy of trusteeship, or the like, all of which ought to figure prominently in an argument that purports to indicts nationalism for its marriage of Reason to capital."(282)

Conclusion: History 1 and History 2, and the New Universals

Subaltern Theory is indeed a very important and radical attempt to provide a critical optic in the formation of postcolonial theory. Its contribution can never be diminished and that is why one expected an expansive and right spirited reaction on Chatterjee's part to take the debate forward but instead of providing new furrows, Chatterjee seems to foreclose all possibilities of opening up the debate through explorations of future theoretic alliances. Chibber reminds us that the present geo-political conjuncture calls for newer approaches to universal models and Chatterjee is certainly not averse to that, but he (Chatterjee) still invokes the foreclosed Europe/Other (History 1/History 2) binary while conceding the necessity of universals. We can end the debate by quoting what Slavoj Zizek, one of the Europe "designated avant gardes" whom Chatterjee debars to speak on matters non-European has to say on the idea of the universal in his essay, "A Leftist Plea for Eurocentrism".

Again, the crucial point here is that subjectivity and universalism are not only not exclusive but are, rather, two sides of the same coin. It is precisely because class struggle interpellates individuals to adopt the subjective stance of a proletarian that its appeal is universal, aiming at everyone with no exceptions. The division it mobilizes is not the division between two well-defined social groups but the division, which runs "diagonally" to the social division in the Order of Being, between those who recognize them-selves in the call of the Truth-Event, becoming its followers, and those who deny or ignore it. In Hegelese, the existence of the true Universal (as opposed to the false concrete universality of the all-encompassing global Order of Being) is that of an endless and incessantly divisive struggle; it is ultimately the division between the two notions (and material practices) of universality, that which advocates the positivity of the existing global Order of Being as the ultimate horizon of knowledge and action, and that which accepts the efficiency of the dimension of the Truth-Event irreducible to (and unaccountable in the terms of) the Order of Being. (Zizek, 1998, 1003)

REFERENCES

Chibber, Vivek., *Postcolonial Theory and the Specter of Capital*, London: Verso, 2013.

Chatterjee, Partha, "Subaltern Studies and Capital", *Economic and*

Political Weekly, September, 14, Vol. XLVIII, No. 37, pp. 69-75, 2013.

Guha, Ranajit, ed., "Dominance without Hegemony" in *Subaltern Studies*, Vol. 6, New Delhi: Oxford University Press, 1989.

Purakayastha, Anindya Sekhar, Review of *Postcolonial Theory and the Specter of Capital*, Vivek Chibber, *Journal of Postcolonial Writing*, Vol. 50, Issue 3, 2014.

Watson, Matthew C, "The Poverty of Postcolonial Theory?", *Postcolonial Studies*, Vol. 16, No. 2, 2013.

Zizek, Slavoj, "A Leftist Plea for Eurocentrism", *Critical Inquiry*, Vol. 24, No. 4, 1998.

10

Critical Amnesia and the Colonizing Semiotic Capital: Can Popular Culture Speak?

This chapter offers a critique of existing theoretic claims of Cultural Studies. It argues that some of the basic tenets of Cultural Studies need to undergo radical revision or reformulation in today's neoliberal context of over-fetishism and corporate enslavement. It engages with recent cultural texts like Bollywood films and popular television reality shows to launch a deconstructive reading of popular cultural theories. In a way therefore, this chapter is an attempt to retheorize cultural studies by underlining the deficit of its existing theoretic templates. Jurgen Habermas has argued that we are today witnessing a refeudalization of the public sphere which is dominated by empirico-analytical sciences with its techno-capitalist imbrications of monological knowledge and culture. Our reified every day praxis today has undergone the process of *diremption* or (*Entzweiung*) which diagnoses a schism within human faculties and human society. Post-globalization, this process of *diremption* has intensified further and our capacity for communicative rationality (*Vernunft*) is now reduced to mere instrumental rationality (*Verstand*). The Hegelian notion of *sittlichkeit* or a organized/harmonized society is a distant dream today. The Culture Industry according to Habermas has caused further colonization of the life-world. Enlightenment claims of universal pragmatics and the autarkical sphere of auratic *avant garde* art are now being accused of elitism and totalitarianism in the contemporary parlance. The postmodern annihilation of the distinction between the high and the low in the name of polysemy and paralogy has paved the way for post-auratic public or popular culture. The pure gaze of elite aestheticism is claimed to have been replaced by *grounded aesthetics* of public culture. Neo-Gramscian revisionism has questioned the concept of the consumer as cultural dupes—a concept which establishes economic reductionism by denying any agency to the culture citizen/consumer. *Soi disant* culturalists are of the view that popular culture is actually resistant and it has a Bakhtinian Carnivalesque potential of heterogeneity and polyphony of democratic dissonance. In other words, popular culture is viewed as tantamount to empowerment and agency. I will show how such pro-popular culture ideological positions have been usurped by the market to generate unbridled commodity fetishism and kitsch aspirations in the name of popular culture. Given that, the question arises, can popular culture really speak? The pro-consumption theory of popular culture treats the cultural site as a semiotic/symbolic field of hermeneutic empowerment, agency and resistance. The cultural text is believed to empower the consumer with free-floating episteme (textual poaching) and semiotic capital. But does the fringe sub-culture really speak through popular culture, or it gets further colonized under the hegemonic and homogenized illusion of mass culture? In other words, is Cultural theory spawning critical amnesia? This chapter engages with this critical cultural inquiry.

For a long time theorists have accorded popular culture a normative status. Advocates of popular culture have justified its validity claims in the name of empowerment and polysemy. Emboldened by postmodern theories, advocates of popular culture have done away with the hiatus between high/elite and low culture as postmodernity has questioned such binarism (Storey, 2001, 168). Promoters of popular culture liquidated such cultural hierarchies in the name of bolstering the fringe. Even the notion of hegemony was also revisited as neologisms like 'semiotic guerrilla warfare', 'secondary production' and 'textual poaching' were doing the rounds to hammer home the fact that market-centric popular culture is not hegemonising. On the contrary popular culture was viewed as potent with its liberating possibilities and it was believed to have equipped the reader/spectator/consumer with emancipatory semiotic capital through which the consumer attains agency and empowerment. Through such agency the consumer is supposed to wage a constant vigil and eternal 'semiotic guerrilla warfare' by which she consumes the text in her own way without being interpellated by the hegemonic designs of the text. While postmodernity boasts of Fiedler's notion of new Gnosticism/new mutants and Susan Sontag's idea of new sensibility (Bertens, 1995, 24-28) which call into question all universal pragmatics of the enlightenment project, is it high time to revisit and interrogate the claims of popular culture theory? The present chapter would like to articulate its enthusiastic participation in the ongoing critical agon by problematizing the validity and justification of popular culture. The question that this chapter will like to pose is, can popular culture speak or whether it has itself become a totalitarian metanarrative subsuming other micronarratives by being completely amnesiac of its rebellious and critical role? Is it colluding with the forces of domination? By popular culture, I refer to market driven mass culture of entertainment. Prominent architects of cultural theory like Stuart Hall and Angela McRobbie have earlier spoken about the emancipatory roles and potentials of popular culture. They believed in creative consumption which entails a process of secondary production by which the consumer/reader would fashion out her own meanings from the text. According to such views, under the approving gaze of cultural theory and postmodernity, the tyrannical visage of the market forces look less hostile and less exploitative. Cultural theory thus spawned a benign image of techno-capitalism. On the contrary, the unitary values of the enlightenment was called oppressive and totalitarian by postmodernity and such univalence was made to yield place to the multivalences of postmodernity and popular culture. But has the ouster of universal metanarratives and elitism resulted in a greater version of seductive totalitarianism and popular elitism? If the Kantian notion of the *sensus communis* (Holub, 1991, 136) was found mistaken by the postmodern theorists and if the Hegelian paradigm of sublation was also treated as abstruse then again the question arises, have we embraced a comprador form of aesthetics when we advocate the death of the aura and the rise of multiperspectivism? All these queries are germane to any reformulation of culture theory. In the post-9/11 world even the future contours of critical theory have been debated. The postmodern championing of groundlessness and dissensus might have led to the reigning glory of relativism and micropolitics, but the post-9/11 world has witnessed the convergence of Habermas and Derrida in 2003 when the two opposing camp-holders of critical theory decided to write a joint draft (Thomassen, 2006, 278-292) where they emphasized the necessity of universal laws and universal values to counter the forces of hegemony. Given this changed scenario when critical theory itself is undergoing a radical paradigm shift, is it not obligatory on our part to refashion and reformulate the basic premises of culture theory? This chapter addresses the need of rethinking and interrogating the claims of popular culture theory by referring to some of the prevalent forms of popular culture in India. I what follows I shall undertake a close reading of a very well known film to unmake the claims of marketized popular culture.

Slumdog Syndrome or Mundania?

The Oscar winning film *Slumdog Millionaire* by Danny Boyle created a lot of critical furor in India and abroad about the film's representational merit. Some are of the view that better films were made before on the same theme in a far better way but those films were not given the Oscar because they were victims of award politics and power games. Such controversies are not the subject of discussion of this chapter but the film *Slumdog Millionaire* is referred here because it gives us a brilliant illustration of a popular phenomenon which for the lack of a more appropriate critical term, I would like to call the slumdog syndrome. The film contains a scene where the celebrated Indian film super star, the Big B (Amitabh Bachchan, the iconic megastar of Bollywood) made a sudden public appearance and is swarmed by hundreds of fans. During this rare public appearance of the Big B, the poor child protagonist of the film finds himself locked in a make shift toilet of a slum where he lives. When the boy came to know about the presence of the superstar in his vicinity, he stopped defecating and wanted to go out to have a look at the star but as someone has mischievously locked him inside the toilet he made frantic efforts to break the toilet door. When all his efforts were in vain the boy's craze for the superstar *darshan* (meet) grew so overpowering that it outweighed his sense of sanity and he decided to use the only escape route available to him (or the culturally liberating/libidinal route?), i.e. the ditch below the make shift toilet in which the shit (excreta) gets stored. He hesitated initially before doing the unthinkable and then jumped into the pool of shit. Smeared with yellow shit he swam and came out into the liberated zone of celebritydom where the cine icon was giving his autographs to his fans. The child's jump into the pool of shit to get a glimpse of the superstar may sound bizarre, exaggerated and a bit overdone but it encapsulates the seduction and craze of the popular culture icons for the dispossessed. Whether such irrational dynamism and kinetic zeal is liberating or emancipatory or regressive and bizarre merit serious critical debate. This scene is one of the most talked about scenes of the film where the bare bodied boy, all smeared in yellow shit runs towards the superstar for an autograph. The absurdity and the brazenness of the entire incident are forgotten under the pervasive and fanatic ethos of Fandom. In popular culture theory, fandom is viewed as freedom and some theorists would equate fan *jouissance* with issues of identity and empowerment. But is it really possible to identify the (fan)atic with the critique? If the Kantian notion of the *sensus communis* (Holub, 1991, p. 136) is viewed as tyrannical then is it to be replaced by this compulsive enslavement of senselessness? The Lyotardian concept of the *differend* questions all universalities and overarching metanarratives (Malpas, 2003, p. 24) but even if one assumes that grand narratives are totalitarian and overmastering, does it mean that they are to be subsumed by the micrologies of slumdog syndromes? The term 'Mundania' (Storey, 2001) suggests a contrast to the supposed liberating dynamism of Fandom. According to theorists like, Fiske and Cartieu, Fandom is redolent with excitement and libidinal empowerment whereas non-fan-mundania is mundane and drab and non-empowering (Storley, 2001,p.176). Pro-fan theories of 'secondary production' and 'creative/resistant consumption' negates the possibility of domination or usurpation and validates the emphasis on receptive mechanisms like secondary production of a cultural text by the reader/consumer. So any view of regarding the consumer as a passive cultural dupe is vehemently opposed by pro-fan theorists as reductive. This mechanism of valorizing the popular is bound to look contrived when set against incidents of slumdog syndrome. Whether we spontaneously articulate our desires and consents for the sites of consumption or whether there is a mechanism for the manufacture of consent can be debated. In fact the postmodern claims of multivalences and liquidation of unitary and universal pragmatics are belied by the seductive totalitarianism of popular culture and the associated media circus. Is popular culture in its attempt to annihilate all grand narratives, itself becoming a metanarrative ? The hermeneutics of life have already been replaced by the erotics of life in the parlance of popular culture, and still there are talks of gaining semiotic capital through a semiotic guerrilla warfare by the cultural consumer. In spite of the apparent hegemonic designs of the culture industry, pro-fan theory is of the view that the consumer is free to internalize the cultural text in her own ways and through this semiotic appropriation of the cultural text the consumer/fan gains semiotic capital which leads to her empowerment and identity formation and liberation. This leads to the idea of Textual Poaching. Both these pro-marketized popular culture views are however problematized if we set them against events of slumdog syndrome which is clearly enslaving and dis-empowering.

Textual Poaching and Neo-Hegemony

Advocates of popular culture endorse the potential claims of individual agency vis-à-vis popular culture by reformulating the hegemony theory. Such revisionary hegemonial concept would repose a lot of faith on individual agency and the power of polysemy. The cultural text is viewed by such revisionary theorists as an open field for individual exploration and appropriation. The site of the cultural text therefore is a domain of free floating signifiers and negating any fixed transcendental signified the cultural consumer becomes a textual poacher (Storey, 2001, p.180) to gather whatever meaning he/she can gather through her unconstrained textual poaching of the cultural text. Such theoretical fanfare about the possibility of semiotic guerrilla warfare or the possibility of subverting the colonial/hegemonial intentions of the textual structure for our own benefit, i.e. Calibanizing the Prosperoian design, may prove to be illusory. One may illustrate recent cases of Indian popular culture like *Dance India Dance* and other such Reality Shows or even Bollywood itself to negate the claims of textual poaching and semiotic guerrilla warfare theories. Programs like *Dance India Dance* may give us the impression that suddenly the whole Indian nation has found its path to emancipation through the kinetic celebration of the body and the libido. Cine experts and Bollywood aficionados go ga ga about the immense potential of empowerment through such popular programs. The judges in these programs would inundate the participants by their programmed appreciative catch phrases like, "mind blowing", "fabulous", "superb", etc. If we watch television shows in the prime time slots we may have a feeling that the whole Indian nation is on a dancing spree and gyrating hips and projected midriffs are the new categorical imperatives of popular liberation. From the dancing zone of reality show studios to the macabre zone of honour killing or forceful disrobing of an adivasi woman by the village panchayat or the intervention of the supreme court to validate same caste marriage in India speak of a different guerrilla warfare. It is a warfare which exposes the naked shingles of corporate designs of the reality shows and it is a warfare which signifies again the fact that real poaching/liberation does not emanate from the mind blowing performance of the dancer but from the constant guerrilla warfare between the forces of hegemony/corporatization and individual/collective critic. The seeming empowerment of the individual through reality shows are having a drugging and benumbing effect on the populace. Media reports corroborate the fact that mega cities in India have recently witnessed mushrooming of dancing schools which are training kids from their infancy about the intricacies of Bollywood dancing so that a prospective kid can outsmart her compatriot on the reality show stage. Everyone has the right to dance and to compete, and no one can rob him/her that constitutional right but problem arises only when that right is made into a universal fetish to be practiced by everyone and such validation of the popular is made to be seen as normative. The binarism of the performative and the pedagogic can be problematized in this context. In the Indian Reality Show context, is the performative/ludic itself becoming pedagogic? Is there a possibility that the micrologies of counter-mechanisms/poaching/semiotic guerrilla warfare are themselves becoming pedagogic and totalitarian? Under the blinding effect of a seemingly benign techno-capitalism which spawns theories of secondary production/creative consumption are we being made to embrace some form of seductive totalitarianism which operates on manufactured consent and false notion of resistance hypothesis? Stuart Hall's edited work, *Resistance Through Rituals: Youth Subculture in Post-War Britain* contains many essays which are unanimous on the point that youth culture "arises out of and cannot be understood apart from the way in which young people translate the problematic of their class position into symbolic forms which...subvert the cultural authority of the dominant social class". (Schwartz, 1978). Such positioning in favour of a popular resistant culture can be seriously questioned now in today's neo-liberal conditions. In the subsequent section I shall elaborate this point further.

Spectacle Pedagogy/Narcissistic Pathology

Keeping in mind the above discussion, the question arises whether we are getting critically amnesiac in the name of empowerment. Is popular culture theory running the risk of colluding with the forces of domination? If we are gaining semiotic capital through our engagement with popular culture the question remains, is there a constant process of the refeudalization of the semiotic capital? Is cultural theory today not alive to the continuous colonization of the lifeworld (Outhwaite, 1994, p.82)? Are we today more than ever before under the "monocular regime of spectacle seduction"(Garoian and Gaudelieus, 2004, p.299)? Spectacle pedagogy today functions as an insidious, ever present form of propaganda in the service of cultural imperialism which has succeeded in constituting the Marcusian "one dimensional" being (Marcuse, 1972, 24-25). The lure of cultural spectacle today has generated a form of narcissistic pathology. Images rule, they also colonize,

> In a society dominated by the production and consumption of images, no part of life can remain immune from the invasion of spectacle. (Lasch, 1991, 122)

> The spectacle is the acme of ideology, for in its full flower it exposes and manifests the essence of all ideological systems: the

> impoverishment, enslavement and negation of real life. (Debord, 1967/1994, 151)

Cultural studies was supposed to have a political stance against such forces of domination, but unfortunately in the Indian context if we continue to employ Western yardsticks and ludic postmodern standpoints then there is greater chance of collusion with the hegemonic structures of culture industry. The advocates of fandom has failed to see the hidden structure of economic coercion imposed by the culture industry. The cultural critic Siegfried Kracauer conceptualized the spectacle of visual culture as "the mass ornament"(Kracauer, 1995) and by comparing the capitalist production process with that of mass ornament he has laid bare the inability of culture study theory to see through the game of capitalism which interpellates the subject in such a way that the hysteric craze of fans for market induced images are viewed as empowerment and identity formation. The Foucauldian notion of the tyrannical panopticon is being replaced today by the synopticon of self-invited hegemony. The seductive charm and compulsive adherence to the appeal of the image is so overbearing that it has spawned a self-validating ideology of commodity culture which generates such overmastering titillation amounts to the "Pavlovian" in its evocation of mass response (Garoian and Gaudelieus, 2004). Such titillations obviously inscribe our "narcissus fixation" with the cultural spectacle and occludes our critical understanding of the spectacle craze as commodity fetishism (McLuhan, 1964, 33). This re-reading of the cultural industry in today's context exposes the inadequacy of pre-existing cultural theories to understand the real forces of the market that generate false consciousness of empowerment. This brings me to focus more on the phenomenon of the spectacle as described by Guy Debord, a phenomenon that colonizes the entire life-world of the new millennium. In what follows I would show how such cultural colonization is creating a society of control.

Informatized Techno-Capitalism/Infoglut/Cultureglut/ Society of Control

Guy Debord's manifesto like aphorisms in *The Society of the Spectacle* were written "with the deliberate intention of doing harm to spectacular society" (Debord, 1994, 10). Such remarks illustrate his vigilant and resistant positioning to expose, examine and critique the acculturation of socially and historically constructed symbolic representations and dispositions of spectacle culture, the *habitus* against which Bourdieu suggests one has to "situate oneself within 'real activity'. Bourdieu's concept of the real is not that of Reality TV where fame seekers are paid to perform bizarre, and often emotionally and physically dangerous feats on television shows. The trivialized notion of reality and thrill in these shows represents an extreme case of commodity fetishism, an insatiable appetite for gazing at others who perform trivialities to titillate our hunger for constant excitement and entertainment. For Jagodzinski such desires for vicarious thrills and cheap entertainment valorizes the "jouissance" which creates fertile condition for late capitalism by constituting "subversive and destabiliosed (multiple and fluid) identities who seek new modes of entertainment and enjoyment (Jagodzinski, 2003). According to Bourdieu, such pleasured, internalized dispositions and idealisms of the social world impelled by visual culture represents a social reality that is consistent with Barthes's characterization of mythic power which depoliticizes critical speech. For Baudrillard the unidirectional gaze of the Panopticon is no longer a fitting metaphor for television. Given that its simulation now precedes reality, "we no longer watch TV, it is TV that watches us" (Baudrillard, 1994, 29).The paradoxical crisis of reality TV is its inducement of the feeling of "being there without being there". Such inducements abolish participatory citizenship by blurring the distinction between our passive and active involvement in society. Are we therefore heading towards a stage where we have allowed ourselves to be controlled by the logic of the 24x7 Reality TV sphere? Are we all adhering to the dictates of a society of control where the citizens are self-induced info-gluts and culture-gluts? How does popular culture theory situate itself in such a scenario where the consumer is made to valorize the ugly visage of capitalism as the savior and harbinger of emancipation? Looking at recent trends of Indian Reality Shows can we really theorize and claim that these cultural forms are empowering the masses or the masses have the ability to appropriate the claptraps of the corporate culture for their own benefit through their engagement with such popular forms of culture? These are valid questions and Cultural Studies in its existing form fail to answer them properly. In what follows I shall explicate this further.

Valid Strip Tease/Neo-Mahabharata/Death of the Aura

"Police to probe Akshay Kumar's 'unbutton' act"
The Times of India, March 30, 2009

Another flawed and delusional narrative popularized by postmodernity is that the popular is always the non-elite and the terms like obscene and vulgar are relative. While I concede that the idea of relativism has significant validity, I continue to inquire whether our market-driven liquidation of the distinction between the high and the low has happened because of the postmodern ethos of paralogy. Prominent advocates of such postmodern paradigm of popular culture that does away with the distinction between the high and the low are critics like Angela McRobbie. In this section I shall expose the limitations of her theoretic claims by engaging with her own works. Her book *Postmodernism and Popular Culture* (1994) has voiced her opinion about the new socio-cultural realm marked by the increasing dominance of the image. McRobbie argues that "this new instantaneity, ubiquity and self-referentiality of culture opens up new possibilities for participation and resistance" (Gottlieb, 1996, 16). Talking about consumerist youth popular culture McRobbie felt that the category of the youth does not exhibit a coherent politics but they voice their innerscape through "structures of feeling" that get played out through consumptions and new cultural forms.(Gottlieb, 1996, 17). Avant garde art/culture has been seen as essentialist and highbrow by postmodern theorists like McRobbie and their consistent validation of the consumption-appropriation-emancipation hypothesis has led to the theoretical cul-de-sac which may inspire us to come out with some incoherent structures of feelings when we witness the Indian cine star,(a term that can be problematized) Akshay Kumar went down the ramp to ask his wife to unzip him before the spectators. Any hue and cry of obscenity over this unprecedented (no longer) incident may be silenced by the advocates of postmodern popular culture theory as retrogressive and foudationalist. If we are to believe McRobbie, perhaps today's youth are expected to gain "some structures of feelings" out of such public unzipping act. They may acquire some libidinal kineticism and identity by blurring the categorical distinction between the high and the low, the debased and the aesthetic, the macabre and the normative but does it amount to emancipation or greater subservience to market forces? There is no taker for *Bildung* or formative aesthetics today (Outhwaite, 1994, 123). Such brouhaha over the triumph of dissensus which legitimizes pornography and public strip tease as valid may inspire us of thinking about a *Neo-Mahabharata* where Draupadi's trauma during her forceful disrobing would have to be reformulated and rethought. If we go by popular culture theory then there cannot be anything ignoble in Draupadi's discomfiture as narrated by the Mahabharata. We attach value to spontaneous strip tease today and we justify it in the name of postmodern multi-perspectivism. For the youth in India today Bollywood is India's Sistine Chapel and the shopping malls are the powerhouses where shopping leads to their empowerment. Apart from that the social networking sites enable them to exchange courtesies with their friends in

New York (communication revolution!)while the outcry of a *Dalit* woman being killed through honor killing verdicts is too weak to get access to Facebook/SMS portals. The postmodern inheritance of popular culture theory, I would argue, needs serious revision to reorient theory so that the talk of activism and political resistance can really materialize.

Paradigm Shift in Culture Theory? New Multitude Culture?

There is a growing demand for a reformulation of culture study theory. The existing theory denigrates any idea of Hegelian sublation through culture. The emphasis is rather on just chilling out through modes of personal hedonist *nirvana*. Zizek in his book, *The Parallax View* (2009) has defined the new age super ego as perpetual hedonism (Zizek, 2006). Keeping in mind the works of Rey Chow, Negri and Hardt and paying heed to the post 9/11 Derrida Habermas convergence (Borradori,2009), an attempt can be made to refashion and revisit the axioms of existing cultural theory. Can there be a third world centric approach to culture theory? Is it possible to explore further the notion of the public sphere to capitalize the potential of mass participation for resistance and social change through public culture? If participation is crucial then why have we ignored the normative potential of the public sphere vis-à-vis popular culture? Inter-subjective communicative action and a meaningful participation of the public sphere can really bring out the dormant potential of the multitude. A radical public sphere theory can explore the possibility of the existence of a coercion free public domain (Johnson, 1994). The multitude can thrive in the age of Empire only when they are made to realize their potential through biopolitics. Negri floated the concept of the *dis-ustopia* which suggests a new sense of creative transformation in a world closed by the clutch of empire and globalization. Real postmodernism would be really empowering for the multitude but for that to happen there has to be a constant sense of ontological exasperation in the multitude. Negri used the term, Kairos, which he says signifies the creative moment of biopolitical transformation (Negri, 2007). Art and culture in the age of empire has to have a dimension of biopolitical transformation. The new dynamics of popular culture theory must converse with such ideas of biopolitics. Popular culture theory is believed to have represented the sub-culture and the fringe voice, and therefore, it is supposed to be anti-hierarchical, but can marginalized culture really speak through popular culture? Is there a hegemony of the popular then? Can we replace it by a neo-ethics as described by Badiou, Naomi Klein, George Monbiot? The fictitious concept of semiotic capital ushered in by the monster metanarratives of the market can be subverted only when we recognize the necessity of a neo-cultural study theory (Hall and Birchall, 2006). The good news is the old die hard voices are softening. McRobbie has already admitted the necessity of a change:

> Indeed I have changed my position quite dramatically, if you can get hold of my new book *The Aftermath of Feminism* you will see how and why it is not that I totally reverse more that I wanted at the time to challenge the over pessimistic Marxists mostly men and to point to how young women were able to use popular culture now I see that popular culture learnt how to re-manipulate young women wanting to be 'empowered' so now they do it for a consumer capitalism which is ruthless and aggressive and not acting in the interest of women at all! (McRobbie, 2010)

The deliberations in today's public sphere can centre on countering the illusory appeal of *laissez faire* evangelism vis-à-vis popular culture. There has to be a new ontology of the new world or for the community to come (Hall and Birchall, 2006, p.3).The debate of the hour again is whether we verge towards convulsive Dionysianism or embrace the unitary matrixes of culture? Post 9/11 clamor for 'Kant after ground zero' is relevant. For the Homo sound-bytes and Homo Silicons of the *fin de millenaire,* attachment for a comprador culture has estranged her from praxis. Theory therefore has become amnesiac of its theoretical commitments to cognitive mapping and counter mechanisms to corporatization. Before further refeudalisation takes place, popular culture theory needs perhaps a complete restructuring. The real mission for culture theory therefore should be to fashion an *Asthetick des Widerstands* i.e. aesthetics of resistance (Holub, 1991, 137).The Baudelairian *flaneur* had a quest for meaning but the *flaneur* ran the risk of leading to the *dandyisme*, the self-fashioner in the Nietzschean sense where society is viewed as *Gesmtkunstwerk* (a spectacular world waiting to give shape to our will to power) waiting to enable the present day dandy/flaneur/ consumer(?) to attain autonomy of choice/consumption (Norris, 1993, p.63). Existing culture study theory perhaps talks about that the vindication of that autonomy, however in the chaos of that autonomy we are losing sight of *Ideologie kritik* which is the ultimate goal of culture theory.

REFERENCES

Baudrillard, J. *Simulacra and Simulation*, Ann Arbor: The University of Michigan Press, 1994.

Borradori, G. *Philosophy in a Time of Terror*. Chicago and London: University of Chicago Press, 2009.

Bertens, H. *The Idea of the Postmodern*, London: Routledge, 1995.

Debord, G. *The Society of the Spectacle*, New York: Zone, 1994.

Gottlieb, J. "Review of Postmodernism and Popular Culture", *Contemporary Sociology*, 25, 1, pp. 16-18, 1996.

Garoian, Charles R, Gaudelius, Y. "The Spectacle of Visual Culture", *Studies in Art Education*, 45, 4, pp. 298-312, 2004.

Hall,G, Birchall, C. *New Cultural Studies, Adventures in Theory*, Hyderabad: Orient Black Swan, 2006.

Holub, R. *Jurgen Habermas*, London; Routledge, 1991.

Johnson, J. "Public Sphere, Postmodernism and Polemic", *The American Political Science Review*, 88, 2, pp. 427-433, 1994.

Jagodzinski, J. "Unromancing the Stone of "resistance"", *Journal of Social Theory in Art Education*, 23, 104-139, 2003.

Kracauer, S. *The Mass Ornament: Weimer Essays*, Cambridge: Harvard University Press, 1995.

Lasch, C. *The Culture of Narcissism: American Life in an Age of Diminishing Expectations*, New York: W.W. Norton, 1991.

Marcuse, H. *One Dimensional Man*, London: University of California Press, 1972.

McLuhan, M. *Understanding Media: The Extensions of Man*, New York: Signet Press, 1964.

Malpas, S. *Routledge Critical Thinker Series on Jean Francois Lyotard*, London: Routledge, 2007.

McRobbie, A. Email Correspondence with the author, 2010.

Negri, A. "Art and Culture in the Age of Empire and the Time of the Multitudes", *SubStance*, 36, 1, pp. 48-55, 2007.

Norris,C. *The Truth about Postmodernism*, Cambridge: Blackwell, 1993.

Outhwaite, W. *Habermas, A Critical Introduction*, Cambridge: Polity, 1994.

Schwartz, G. "Review of Resistance Through Rituals", *The American Journal of Sociology*, 84, 3, pp.789-791, 1978.

Storey, J. *Cultural Theory and Popular Culture*, England: Pearson, 2001.

Thomassen, L. *The Derrida Habermas Reader*, Chicago: Chicago University Press, 2006.

Index